FRANSEN NO A

INSIDE THE MIND
OF A TEEN KILLER

PHIL CHALMERS

THOMAS NELSON
Since 1798

NASHVILLE   DALLAS   MEXICO CITY   RIO DE JANEIRO   BEIJING

Published in Nashville, Tennessee, by Thomas Nelson. Thomas Nelson is a registered trademark of Thomas Nelson, Inc.

Unless otherwise noted, Scripture quotations are taken from the HOLY BIBLE, NEW INTERNATIONAL VERSION.® © 1973, 1978, 1984 by International Bible Society. Used by permmission of Zondervan Publishing House. All rights reserved.

Thomas Nelson, Inc., titles may be purchased in bulk for educational, business, fund-raising, or sales promotional use. For information, please e-mail SpecialMarkets@ThomasNelson.com.

Library of Congress Control Number: 2009923244

ISBN: 978-1-59555-977-7

Printed in the United States of America

09 10 11 12 13 QW 5 4 3 2 1

CONTENTS

This book is dedicated to the victims and families of teen killers, and to children and teenagers who are victims of abuse and bullying. I pray this project improves the lives of children everywhere.

FOREWORD

We are living in the most violent times in recorded peacetime history.

Medical technology saves more lives than ever before, preventing more deaths of victims of attempted murders every year. But the rate at which our citizens are *trying* to kill each other may well be the highest in recorded peacetime history.

A study published by the University of Massachusetts and Harvard University in 2002 demonstrated that if we had 1970s-level medical technology today, the murder rate would be three to four times what it is. In other words, three out of four deaths from attempted murders today are prevented by the advances in medical technology in just the last thirty years.

If we had 1930s-level evacuation, transportation, and medical technology (no automobiles or telephones for most people, and no antibiotics), the murder rate would probably be at least ten times what it is today. If we had 1870s frontier-level medical technology (no cars, no phones, no antibiotics, no antiseptics, and no anesthesia), the rate at which we would be successful at killing each other could be fifteen times what it is now.

We live in times that make the violence of the Old West pale by comparison. This explosive increase in the serious assault rate can be seen in every major industrialized nation around the world. We are living in tragically violent times, and there is every reason to believe that it is going to get worse.

What our children are doing in the high schools and the middle schools today predicts what they will be doing as adults in our communities and our workplaces in the years to come. The kids who gave us Jonesboro in the middle school and Columbine in the high school are now giving us mall massacres, workplace massacres, and college massacres—like Virginia Tech.

In this tragic, violent new age, it has never been more important to study and understand the roots of violence. If our civilization is going to survive, we must study and *master* the violence within our children and our society. And that is exactly what this book is all about.

Phil Chalmers has interviewed the killers. He has corresponded with them extensively. He has exhaustively researched their crimes. There is no human being alive who knows more about these killers, and as you read this book, he will truly take you *Inside the Mind of a Teen Killer.*

Phil has written a book that involves the reader in the unraveling of a mystery—namely, why these kids became killers. And, most importantly, what we can do to stop the killing—*if* anyone is willing to listen. And we *must* listen. Our future and our survival depend upon it.

So let us study and learn from this book. And let us pray that we can use the information here to save lives, prevent more murders, and turn the tide of violence in our civilization.

— DAVE GROSSMAN
Lt. Col., U.S. Army (ret.)
Director, Killology Research Group
(www.killology.com)
Author of *On Killing, On Combat,*
and *Stop Teaching Our Kids to Kill*

Phil (right) pictured with murder expert Lt. Col. Dave Grossman, who wrote the foreword of this book. Lt. Col. Grossman has made a huge impact on Phil's writing and speaking career and is a big inspiration to him.

INTRODUCTION

In Michael Newton's book *Killer Kids,* he tells how during the carefree 1950s, former FBI director J. Edgar Hoover "warned Congress and the nation at large of a startling new menace, ranked second only to godless Communism as a critical threat to life, liberty, and the American way. A new crime wave was brewing . . . spawned from a 'juvenile jungle' whose denizens drove hot rods, dressed in leather jackets, and kept switchblades at the ready, anxious to 'rumble' with any and all corners." He was talking about the growing threat of teen violence almost five decades ago—a problem that today is getting out of control and deserves our undivided attention.

I did not write this book to glorify crime or to sensationalize these unfortunate tragedies. I have no hidden agenda, and I didn't write it just to make a quick buck.

I wrote this book with only one thing in mind—change. My hope is that the research and studies I have compiled during the last two decades can create positive change; educate law enforcement, youth workers, teachers, and parents about warning signs in potentially violent teens; and hopefully save many innocent lives.

What sets this book apart from the many other crime books is the multitude of firsthand crime accounts by dozens of teen killers. You could say that I have cowritten this book with more than two hundred inmates who killed when they were teens, in addition to a handful of other high-profile serial killers and mass murderers.

These offenders will explain what led up to their crimes, what they were thinking about during their crimes, and what motivated them to commit such terrible horrors. More importantly, they will explain how they could have been stopped and will offer warning signs that any person paying attention could have noticed.

When I was a kid in Cleveland, Ohio, in the sixties, we lived in a not-so-nice urban section of town. Our neighborhood was so crime-ridden and corrupt that one of our burglars was even a police officer. My dad held him at gunpoint until the "good" police came to remedy the situation. When I was ten years old, my brother and I were robbed at knifepoint on our way to school. My parents finally decided it was time to move, and we escaped to the suburbs.

After graduating from high school, I gave college a shot and attended Kent State University in Ohio. It wasn't my cup of tea, so I changed direction and started working with young people at a juvenile prison. I had been a pretty bad role model to my peers growing up and had led others down the wrong path of sex, drugs, alcohol, and trouble. I felt it was time that I repaid society for some of the wrong I had done, so I traveled to the youth prison every week and started personally connecting with the locked-up young men.

This experience influenced me so much that I decided to devote my life to helping young people steer clear of the destructive life of crime. My expertise over the years has been in youth culture, youth entertainment, and helping teens avoid destructive behavior. I have studied related subjects like teen sex, STDs, drug and alcohol abuse, drunk driving, suicide, teen violence, school violence, and crime prevention. I speak to teens, write books, and help guide students, teachers, police, parents, and youth workers in the right direction.

As I passionately pursued my investigation of youth culture, each time I heard or read about a school shooting or a teen murder, I wondered what exactly led those young persons to commit such atrocities. I asked the same questions as everyone: *What were they thinking? Why did they choose murder as a solution? What led to their crimes? Could we have stopped them if we had reached them in time?* As I watched news reports flash commentary after commentary from so-called "experts," I became disheartened and dissatisfied, since they could not provide any reasonable answers or glimpses of hope. I decided that one day I would intensely study this problem and report my findings to educate our nation.

When I began my research of teen murder, I quickly realized that if I were to truly determine why young people were violently ending innocent lives, I needed to speak directly to them. I began to correspond with these men and women, detailing the project I was undertaking and telling them what I hoped to learn from their experiences. This book includes many of the things I've discovered during this eye-opening process.

The two most significant and juxtaposing things I have learned about teen murderers are how violent they can be and—at the same time—how normal they can seem. Some of these murders are as violent and gruesome as the horrific crimes committed by psychotic serial killers. Yet some of these teen killers appear to be normal and balanced young people who were raised in loving and stable families. They are your average, next-door-neighbor-type kids who date your daughter and play soccer with your son. They are the quiet teenagers who attend class at the local high school and may even cut your grass and feed your pets while you are on vacation. Some of them have such an above-average intelligence that they could have been valedictorians of their graduating classes!

My hope and prayer is that this book will help to save young people in our own families and communities—one person at a time. We all need to work together to look for warning signs of potentially violent kids and find help for them before it's too late. You may save a neighbor's life, the lives of kids at a local school, or even the life of your own child.

If you would like to get more information about teen murder, to obtain additional resources, or to contact me, log on to my Web site, www.PhilChalmers.com.

Phil on death row, in the mid-1980s, with Oklahoma teen killer and former Satanist Sean Sellers, who was executed in 1999 for shooting to death his parents and a convenience store clerk.

ONE

CHURCH KID SLAUGHTERS FAMILY—NEWS AT ELEVEN

Good wombs hath born bad sons.

—WILLIAM SHAKESPEARE,
The Tempest, quoted by Eric Harris and Dylan Klebold,
Littleton, Colorado, school shooters

Luke Woodham called himself a social reject. He was the product of a painful divorce. A victim of clinical depression as a child. A casualty of merciless bullying. An angst-ridden teenager whose first and only love had shattered his heart.

On the outside, Luke resembled the average teenager. On the inside, he was a dormant volcano. What catapulted sixteen-year-old Luke into a violent rage on October 1, 1997, in the small town of Pearl, Mississippi, where he bashed his mother to death with a baseball bat, shot two classmates to death, and injured seven others? What made this baby-faced young man, who had seemingly typical adolescent problems, erupt in such a volatile fashion?

You may assume that Luke had an unusually dreadful childhood. Maybe you are even suspecting child abuse or sexual molestation—some overly traumatic, life-defining moment that served to create the monster within. But it wasn't just one particular event. Luke was simply overwhelmed by deep, emotional debris that he was never able to process in a healthy way.

Luke remembers his early years in random snapshots. He was born on February 5, 1981, to seemingly normal parents and a bossy older brother. They later acquired a friendly dog named Sparkle. Luke's most disturbing

Journal of Pearl, Mississippi, school shooter Luke Woodham. On this particular page, Luke vows never to be hurt by a girl again and signed the letter in his own blood. He proceeded to murder his mother, his ex-girlfriend, and another female student at the school.

memories are the screaming matches between his mom and dad. They engaged in bitter verbal battles that left a young Luke confused, scared, and most times in tears. On several occasions when his mom tucked him in and kissed him good night, he desperately begged, "When are you guys going to stop fighting?"

She never replied, but the answer came when Luke's father took off one day when Luke was eight years old. He never came back. Luke was convinced

Boyhood home of Pearl, Mississippi, school shooter Luke Woodham, and the site where he murdered his mother with a baseball bat and a butcher knife.

he was at fault and never fully recovered. During the time he should have been playing on a Little League team or joining the Boy Scouts, Luke sank into a deep depression that would last for years. He tearfully told me, "I regretted my birth—even today I still feel guilty."

Luke retreated into a world of solitude. He did what he knew best—read books, daydreamed, and socialized with imaginary friends. He was embarrassed by his looks—his chubby frame, dorky glasses, and buckteeth. He had trouble communicating his emotions, and the only way he knew how to deal with his festering pain and sadness was to draw deeper internally. Though he shut the world out, he was desperate for someone to care. When no one did, Luke sought answers in a place that only fueled and poisoned his silent rage. And there he was pushed over the proverbial edge.

Luke discovered a twisted semblance of solace when he joined a satanic cult in 1996. The cult leader, Grant Boyette, was instrumental in shaping Luke's tormented emotional state by advocating graphic fantasies of death and murder and, specifically, a school shooting. (Grant Boyette was convicted and sentenced to six months at the Parchmoon Boot Camp and five years supervised probation.) On September 30, 1997, Grant convinced Luke it was time to seek revenge for his cruel life by finally acting out his homicidal daydreams. The very next day Luke scribbled what should have been a suicide note. He wrote, "The world s—t on me for the final time."

The following day Luke armed himself with a butcher knife, a baseball bat, and a .30-30 rifle. His mother was his first victim. She died after he

I am not insane! I am angry. This world shunned me for the final time. I am not spoiled or lazy, for murder is not weak and slow-witted, murder is gutsy and daring. I killed because people like me are mistreated everyday. I do this to show society "push us and we will push back."[1] I suffered all my life. No one ever truly loved me. No one ever truly cared about me. I only love one thing in my whole life and that was Christina Menefee. But she was torn away from me. I tried to save myself with Melissa Williams, but she never cared for me. As it turns out, she made fun of me behind my back while we were together. And all throughout my life I was ridiculed. Always beaten, always hated. Can you society, truly blame me for what I do? Yes, you will, the majority of the population, wouldn't be high enough if you did read it, wouldn't make good gossip for all the old ladies. But I shall tell you one thing, I am malicious because I am miserable. The world has beaten me. Wednesday 7, 1997, shall go down in history as the day I fought back. (At this time Grant, say when you will, when you are through, I ask you to read to them sec.123 of the Gay Science in "the madman".)

Grant, see you in the holding cell!

Writings of Pearl, Mississippi, school shooter Luke Woodham, in which he stated "murder is gutsy and daring" and "push and we will push back" and the day he shot up Pearl High School "shall go down as the day I fought back."

(left) *Rear entrance of Pearl High School, where school shooter Luke Woodham exited the building and was quickly apprehended by a teacher and police.*

(right) *Pearl, Mississippi, school shooter Luke Woodham moments after his murder spree at Pearl High School. Police took this photo after they tackled and handcuffed him.*

stabbed her multiple times and beat her with a baseball bat. Luke then drove to his high school and continued his killing spree, ending the lives of two young students, including his ex-girlfriend, and wounding seven others. He thought he'd finally found justice.

"I was just trying to find hope in a hopeless world, man. That's all there is to it. I just wanted a better life for myself, and I've never had one."[1] His "better" life is now being spent behind bars in a Mississippi penitentiary. He will never experience life as a free man again.

It's easy to look at Luke without an ounce of compassion or sympathy. His actions were despicable, inexcusable, and irreparable. Yet something gnaws at my spirit when I wonder how an adolescent who struggled with esteem issues and depression—problems characteristic of many teenagers—could transform into a violent and vengeful murderer. While many teenagers experience some degree of angst or family trouble in their lives, rarely do they resort to murder.

It's difficult to stand back, ask the tough questions, and somehow try to unscramble the mess of a teen killer's mind. It's definitely much easier to quickly condemn them or to blame the parents who "made" them this way. I wrote this book to wrestle with these questions and to shed some light on how we can stop raising violent teenagers.

Luke's story is the foundation of this book. Throughout every chapter, his biography is dissected for you to study his journey toward senseless murder—from his dealings with the occult to his fascination with violent media to his inability to appropriately manage schoolyard bullies.

You may be expecting me to immediately paint an accurate picture of a teen killer or school shooter. But, quite frankly, it is almost impossible. They are white, black, Native American, Asian, and Hispanic. They live in the suburbs and in the inner cities. They come from upper-class, middle-class, and poor families. Some come from balanced and healthy families, and others come from broken homes. Some are religious and others are agnostic. Some are extremely intelligent, and others have very low IQs. The sad truth is that a teen killer could come from your own neighborhood and even from your own family.

A Father's Heartbreak and My Conviction

The title of this chapter, "Church Kid Slaughters Family," refers to teen killer Alex Helgeson of Minnesota. At the time of his offense, he was fourteen years old and had no history of mental illness or substance abuse. When I heard about Alex's story, I was so disturbed that I immediately arranged to meet with the boy's father, Dean Helgeson.

The Helgeson family was a churchgoing family with strong ties to the local community. One night, after Mr. Helgeson came home from a church meeting, his life unexpectedly changed forever. When he walked through the front door, he smelled the distinct stench of gunpowder mixed with the metallic odor of blood. Engulfed by nausea, he entered the living room, and his eyes captured a grisly scene that would be permanently etched in his memory—the bloody carnage of his wife's and their two sons' dead bodies. Suddenly, Mr. Helgeson heard a gunshot echo through the house. He didn't realize then that the sound came from his oldest son, Alex, who had just committed suicide after shooting his own mother and brothers.

Alex regularly attended church, was known as a nice young man who was pleasant to be around, and had a number of close friends. He exhibited no behavioral red flags. Yet Alex clearly struggled with some tumultuous internal issues, and on the day of the murders, he had reached his boiling point.

The ordeal began in his bedroom, where he loaded a hunting rifle with six rounds. He then walked down the hallway toward the living room where his mother, Mary Helgeson, and his brothers—Matthew, twelve, and Marcus, seven—were watching television. Only a few moments later, all three victims lay dead, brutally shot by Alex.

After his vicious rampage, Alex walked upstairs to his bedroom, telephoned his church youth leader, and asked, "How do I get to heaven?" He then proceeded to destroy his vast collection of violent music and video games, smashed his CD player into pieces, and penned a suicide letter on a couple of yellow sticky notes. Alex posted these notes on his father's bed and waited for Mr. Helgeson to come home. When he heard his father walk through the front door, Alex pointed the rifle at his own head and ended his life.

When we hear of a school shooting or of a teenager such as Alex who massacred his own family, we are shocked. We use that as an opportunity to evaluate the health of youth culture. But what about the periods of time between these highly publicized and tragic crimes? How violent are our country's young people?

MURDER—THE NUMBERS

While the general murder rate has fallen in the last twenty years and has seemed to level out in the past few years, this doesn't necessarily mean that violent teen behavior is as stable. The grim statistics, targeted toward teens, reveal that killers are getting younger and younger every year. Twelve-, ten-, and even seven- and eight-year-olds are being arrested for murder.

In 2002, one in twelve murders in the United States involved a juvenile offender, or roughly 8 percent of all reported murders.[2] In 2003, law enforcement agencies made 2.2 million arrests of persons under age eighteen.[3]

Current research exposes a frightfully high level of violent activity in our nation's schools:[4]

- Among teenagers ages five through eighteen there were seventeen school-associated violent deaths between 2005 and 2006.
- In 2005, students ages twelve to eighteen were victims of about 1.5 million nonfatal crimes at school, including thefts and violent crimes.
- Between 2005 and 2006, 86 percent of public schools reported at least one violent crime, theft, or other crime.[5]
- During the same period, there were 14 homicides and 3 suicides of school-age youth.[6]

Lt. Col. David Grossman—a retired army officer, former West Point psychology professor, and best-selling author of the Pulitzer Prize–nominated book *On Killing*—observed that from 1960 through 1991, while the U.S. population increased by 40 percent, violent crime increased by 500 percent (murders increased 170 percent, rapes by 520 percent, and aggravated assaults by 600 percent).[7] Clearly, our nation is getting more violent. Though the murder rate has fallen, it is not necessarily an indication that we are becoming less violent. The violent assault rate is up, for example, and teens are doing a great job of hurting people instead of killing them.

We can examine the simultaneously steady murder rate and escalating wave of teen violence through a number of things, but specifically through the aggravated assault rate, the basic barometer of violence in our country. In legal terms, this is an aggressive form of assault, usually with a deadly weapon. Even in the presence of a steady murder rate, the aggravated assault rate has increased seven times since the 1950s.[8] And there are no signs of it slowing down.

Another item to keep in mind is the advancements that have been made in our medical technology over the years, specifically in the development of lifesaving capabilities. Because of these medical breakthroughs, fewer people are dying from violent attacks. Lt. Col. Grossman asserted that if we used the same technology from the 1870s, the murder rate today would be fifteen times higher. If we used technology from the 1930s, the rate would be ten times higher, and with the use of 1970s technology, four times higher.

The U.S. Medical Service Corps echoed a similar sentiment. In a published report, they claimed that nine out of ten soldiers in the Vietnam War would survive a wound that would have killed nine out of ten soldiers in World War II.[9] While a century ago there was a high probability of death with any significant loss of blood or puncture injury to the abdomen, skull, or lungs, that's not the case today.

Is a falling or level murder rate the result of a decrease in violent incidences, or is it perhaps the result of advancements in the medical field? Lt. Col. Grossman opined that our modern medical technology is holding the rate down. I agree. Don't make the mistake of being comfortable with the false sense of security a steady murder rate might offer. We must not ignore the simple fact that the environment surrounding our children is becoming increasingly violent and, as a result, so are our children.

The Six Types of Teen Killers

From extensive research, interviews with legal and medical professionals and law enforcement officials, and in studying killers one-on-one, I have determined that teen killers generally fall into six categories: the family killer, the school killer/shooter, the gang/cult killer, the crime killer, the baby killer, and the thrill killer.

The Family Killer

This type of criminal kills one or more members of his or her family. In 1996, fourteen-year-old Cody Posey shot and killed his father, his step-mother, and his stepsister on ABC News correspondent Sam Donaldson's New Mexico ranch, where his father served as manager. He was convicted of murder, but was sentenced to a juvenile facility for a maximum of five years. Cody admitted he specifically killed his sister "so she couldn't go tell or nothing."[10]

In 1985, in Buffalo, New York, seventeen-year-old John Justice murdered

NYS DOCS

67B0385
JUSTICE, JOHN
6'3"   220lbs
DATE 8/6/07

John Justice murdered his mother, father, and his younger brother in his family home in Buffalo, New York. He then left in a car and rammed it into a neighbor's car, killing the neighbor. He was trying to commit suicide in the car accident.

his mother, father, and brother by stabbing them to death. As he left the scene of the crime, in an attempt to commit suicide, he rammed his automobile into a neighbor's car, accidentally killing the neighbor. John then called the police and told them to check his home address. He tried to commit suicide a second time by slitting his wrists.

THE SCHOOL KILLER/SHOOTER

The school killer is a unique individual. Many of these kids have a misconception of justice and carry out their crimes as a way to get back at those who have bullied them. Luke Woodham is one example of such revenge kills. "I attacked the other students at random because I believed that they had all wronged me because of the way that I had been picked on and mistreated," Luke told me.

There are several cases that I'm sure most of you are familiar with, including the Columbine massacre in Littleton, Colorado, and the shooting in Paducah, Kentucky. But this isn't a new phenomenon.

One of the first school shootings occurred in 1978, when thirteen-year-old Robin Robinson shot and wounded his principal. Robin had been disciplined and paddled by this man. When Robin was threatened with a second paddling, he went home, retrieved a handgun, and returned to school. He then shot and wounded the principal. Robin spent time in a juvenile facility. After his release, he killed a retired police officer during a burglary and was sent to an adult prison.

January 29, 1979, in San Diego, California, sixteen-year-old Brenda Spencer, the first female school shooter, opened fire in an elementary school across from her home, using a .22-caliber gun that her father had given her for Christmas. The terrifying ordeal lasted for six hours. When it was over, two people were dead and nine others were wounded, including a police officer and eight children.

When Brenda was asked why she committed the crime, her response was nonchalant: "I don't like Mondays. This livens up the day . . . I had no reason for it, and it was just a lot of fun." She compared her crime to "shooting ducks in a pond" and said the victims "looked like a herd of cows standing around, it was really easy pickings."[11]

THE GANG/CULT KILLER

Another kind of teen killer is motivated to kill because of involvement in a gang or cult. I have discovered that young people who live in major urban areas are more inclined to join a gang, while those who live in rural areas or suburban neighborhoods tend to become involved with a cult or hate group. Regardless of the kind of group they join, these troubled kids viciously act on their hatred, skewed religious convictions, or allegiance to a particular group.

In 1995, three young men, part of a white supremacist group—otherwise known as skinheads—killed members of their family in Allentown, Pennsylvania. Eighteen-year-old Ben Birdwell and his cousins—brothers Bryan Freeman, seventeen, and David Freeman, fifteen—lived by KKK principles. Bryan and David's family, however, were practicing Jehovah's Witnesses. One day as the three boys were hanging out in the basement of the Freeman home, Mrs. Freeman and the boys started to argue. As shouts escalated, Bryan grabbed a steak knife and stabbed his mother twice. She died immediately.

After Bryan stuffed a pair of shorts into his mother's mouth, the boys moved upstairs. David and Ben took control and killed Mr. Freeman, smashing his head in with a baseball bat and an ax handle, and finally slicing his throat. They proceeded to bludgeon eleven-year-old Eric, Bryan and David's little brother, with a baseball bat. The boys changed clothes, stole two hundred dollars and the family car, and drove to Michigan to stay at the home of a fellow skinhead. They were soon apprehended, arrested, and convicted of murder. All were sentenced to life in prison.[12]

THE CRIME KILLER

A crime killer is a person who murders during the process of committing another crime, such as a robbery, a drug deal, or a rape. The most common incidences associated with crime killers appear to be sexually based assaults. Many rape victims, for example, are murdered after they are raped, to eliminate them as witnesses.

Rhode Island resident Craig Price, reported to be the youngest serial killer in history, slaughtered four people by his fifteenth birthday. Craig made his first kill at the age of thirteen, and his second, third, and fourth kills in 1989 at the age of fifteen. His victims included two adult women and two children, ages eight and ten. The primary motive in each crime was robbery. When Craig showed up at the homes, he was surprised to find his victims there and believed he had no other option than to kill them.

The *Providence Journal* reported Craig's description of what he had experienced when he plunged the weapon into his first victim: "Panic gave way to anger, and anger gave way to a blinding fury. Some people say it, but I've actually seen it: I could actually see the color red cloud my vision . . . and the rage I felt was like a wave of heat that kept crashing on me and popping my ears."

At his trial, Craig showed little remorse and was convicted of all four homicides. Because he was so young, he was sentenced to a youth facility until his twenty-first birthday. While in prison, he committed numerous other crimes and is now serving a lengthy sentence in an adult prison facility.

THE BABY KILLER

During the last twenty years, there have been numerous cases of teenagers who gave birth, panicked, and killed their newborn infants. While we will not focus much attention on this genre of killers, it is certainly a disconcertingly horrifying criminal act.

In 1996, eighteen-year-olds Amy Grossberg and her boyfriend, Brian Peterson Jr., killed their baby in a hotel in New Jersey. Brian said he "thought the infant was born dead and insisted that his girlfriend begged him to 'Get rid of it!'"[13] The infant was beaten on the head, furiously shaken, stuffed into a garbage bag, and tossed into a dumpster outside the hotel. Police found the body the next day.

When Amy developed complications the day after she gave birth, she was rushed to the hospital. Soon afterward, both teenagers confessed to the crime and were arrested. They were charged with first degree murder and convicted of manslaughter.

THE THRILL KILLER

This criminal kills simply to experience the sheer excitement of the act and to see if he or she can get away with it.

In 2001, seventeen-year-old Robert Tulloch and sixteen-year-old James Parker committed a crime that was labeled as "the Dartmouth Murders." Both boys were very intelligent, loved the outdoors, and didn't use drugs. They developed an intense and overwhelming urge to kill and began looking for the perfect victim. On ABC's television show *Prime Time Live*, James said, "We were gonna be sort of bad a—es, you know . . . if we needed to kill somebody, we would be able to do it."

Robert and James stumbled upon a well-educated and friendly couple, both professors at Dartmouth College, who lived in their town of Hanover, New Hampshire. This sweet couple invited the young men into their home, believing that Robert and James were conducting a survey about nuclear power. Instead, the boys slit the couple's throats, stabbed them to death, and pillaged their home. They were captured in Indiana trying to hitchhike to California.

During the trial it was discovered that both had previously attempted to kill four other people. Robert and James were convicted of first degree murder and sentenced to life in prison without the possibility of parole.

Why do teens kill? What factors combine to produce juvenile killers? In the next chapter, we will further analyze the motives behind these crimes.

FOR MORE INFORMATION ON TEEN MURDER
AND THE CASES COVERED IN THIS BOOK,
LOG ON TO WWW.PHILCHALMERS.COM.
DON'T MISS PHIL'S BOOK,
THE ENCYCLOPEDIA OF TEEN KILLERS.

TWO

REASONINGS WITHIN: WHY TEENS KILL

The thing that impresses me the most about America
is the way parents obey their children.

—KING EDWARD VIII (1894–1972)

The most frequently asked question when I tell someone I'm writing a book
on teen murder is, why do teens kill? In the course of my research, I've discovered answers by people with varying backgrounds, experiences, and voca-
tions. Here is what they have said:

- "Mostly, children are a product of their culture, and in our culture,
  it is the incessant, inescapable drumbeat of media violence, which is
  the new factor feeding the virus of violence."
  — LT. COL. DAVE GROSSMAN,
  author of *On Combat, On Killing,*
  and *Stop Teaching Our Kids to Kill*

- "Teens kill because of the darkness in their hearts, and they have
  accepted violence as normal behavior. Violence is the furthest
  thing from normal."
  — JOE SCHILLACI,
  Miami homicide detective,
  featured on the A&E TV show
  The First 48

- "I believe that teens are killing others today because they are caught in an identity crisis. They try to gain respect from their peers based on an identity that is shaped through video, radio and movies, that is often not attainable or realistic."

  — WISE,

  rap artist, who worked with 2Pac's group the Outlaws

Luke Woodham narrowed his perspective on teen murder to three reasons—exposure to violence, desensitization from said exposure, and a lack of morality. He explained:

Children are so exposed to violence, and violence is so glorified and accepted in the media that they are desensitized to it. It's impossible to watch television for very long now without seeing murders, gunshots, assaults, and rape. Nothing is shocking to the youth of our culture anymore. Children are also desensitized and inspired by the violence that is around them in real life, especially the violence that is committed against them. When children are bullied and abused by their peers or parents, any violence that they express is going to be equal or greater than what they are going through.

Our nation does not have the same level of morality that it has had in times past. We don't believe in a general sense of right and wrong anymore, and we don't hold ourselves accountable for our actions like we used to. The mind-set in our society now is to care only for yourself and your own gratification. When you don't value the life and rights of others, you don't view them as human, making it a lot easier to commit a violent act against them.

I could start rattling off a quick answer or two as to why teens kill, but the truth is the answer isn't so simple. It's not just drugs or the availability of guns or poor parenting. There is no single-cause model. Loyola University psychologist James Garbarino, who has specifically studied school shooters, commented, "It's like a kid piling up a tower of blocks. Eventually, it falls over. You could point to the final block and say, that one's the cause. But it's an accumulation of risk factors."[1]

Take, for example, a teen fascinated with violent video games, which, by itself, may not pose a great risk. If he is, however, physically abused at home, bullied at school, and using drugs, then playing a violent video game or watching a movie may act as the catalyst that causes him to fall over the edge.

I've determined ten common things behind the making of violent and murderous teens.

1. An abusive home life and bullying
2. Violent entertainment and pornography
3. Anger, depression, and suicide
4. Drug and alcohol abuse
5. Cults and gangs
6. Easy access to and fascination with deadly weapons
7. Peer pressure
8. Poverty and criminal lifestyle
9. Lack of spiritual guidance and appropriate discipline
10. Mental illness and brain injuries

Luke Woodham's story has strong roots in bullying, depression, anger, and cults.

> I am the epitome of all Evil! I have no mercy for humanity for they created me, they tortured me until I snapped and became what I am today . . . No one truly loved me. No one ever truly cared about me. I only loved one thing in my whole life and that was Christina Menefee. But she was torn away from me. —from Luke's journal

Luke was a beautiful, blond-headed, blue-eyed child who was intelligent, energetic, and incredibly lovable. He spent a lot of time holed up in his bedroom daydreaming and reading—his two favorite things.

As I wrote in chapter 1, Luke's depression began when he was eight years old, right after his parents split up. It got worse in school, where he was tormented every day for being different, for looking like a "nerd." Because he felt isolated from his mother and didn't have any support from friends or other relatives, he didn't know how to deal with the constant bullying. It was an embarrassing subject to talk about, and Luke didn't feel like there was anyone who would care to listen. When he was nine years old, he and his brother got into a fight. Luke fell down on his bed, kicked his sibling hard against his desk, and started to scream and cry at the top of his lungs, "I wish I was dead! I wish I was dead! I would rather be in hell!"

In high school Luke started making friends. He even fell in love with a young lady named Christina Menefee. Though they only dated a few times, when she stopped dating him, he was beyond heartbroken. The depression that seemed to have temporarily lifted began to overwhelm him once again.

Toward the end of 1996, when Luke was a sophomore in high school, his friend Grant Boyette confided to Luke that he was a Satan worshipper. Luke wasn't quite sure exactly what that meant, but he was curious since he had long harbored a secret fascination with the occult. He didn't feel Satanism was evil or even something to take seriously. It was simply an interesting mystery. One day Grant gave Luke a pentagram drawn on a folded-up piece of paper and told him to use it whenever he needed anything. Then Grant gave Luke specific instructions to get inside a dark room, kneel, put his thumbs on the pentagram, put the symbol to his forehead, and meditate about whatever it was he wanted. Somewhat confused but also drawn, Luke shoved the drawing in his pocket, shrugged his shoulders, and said, "Sure."

A few days later he got the opportunity he didn't even know he was waiting for. His mom was out of town for a few days, and one of Luke's friends, Lucas, was spending some time with him at the Woodham home. Another friend had asked Luke if three of her friends, who had been kicked out of their homes, could crash at Luke's place for a few days. Luke obliged.

In walked Danny, Danny's cousin Rocky, and Nathan. Danny was a troublemaker who was constantly rude and picked on both Luke and Lucas. The other two boys were relatively harmless. One night, after Danny was especially hostile, a fed-up Luke remembered the pentagram and the instructions Grant had given him. He put it to use after his houseguests stepped out for the evening.

Luke nervously walked into his bathroom and opened up the crumpled piece of paper. He followed Grant's instructions and wished that "Danny would go away." Grant came over within the hour, and together they cast some spells from a book called *The Necronomicon.* After the words were spoken, an image immediately popped into Luke's head. It was Rocky. The boys finished casting their spells and Grant went home.

A day later, at about one thirty in the morning, Luke was startled by a knock at the door. Danny stood outside numbly repeating, "Rocky's dead, Rocky's dead." Rocky had been hit by a car while crossing a highway and was instantly killed.

Freaked out by the recent spells, the mental image of Rocky, and now Rocky's sudden death, Luke called Grant. He responded apathetically, "Next time, be more specific." A few days later Grant told Luke of some plans he had been forming. He wanted to start an official Satanist group and suggested that Luke use the pentagram again for guidance and direction. Luke was too curious and too scared not to do it, so he got out the occult symbol and prayed. Almost immediately, he saw another mental picture, this time of two of his friends, Wes Brownell and Alan Shaw. Grant and Luke began to court the boys into their club, and they soon formed "the Kroth."

The mission of this satanic club was simple. Each member had to swear his soul to Satan and spread evil on the earth, whether spiritually or physically. In turn Satan would reveal his plan and purpose for their lives. On numerous occasions Grant would give an order to attack a particular person, and Luke would pray that something bad would happen to him or her. Without fail, every time Luke begged Satan to bring harm on an individual, that person would either get sick, his car would break down, or serious physical harm would befall him.

As time went on, Luke became more and more hate-filled, vengeful, and violent. He was the most isolated he had ever been, and all his mental and emotional energies were devoted to worshipping Satan and serving Grant. Grant took advantage of Luke's devotion and fueled his hatred by reminding Luke of how poorly he was treated and how miserable his life was. He also advocated that the Kroth members create evil plans, and he condemned them for not thinking "more evil."

By the end of the summer, 1997, the Kroth had dissolved back into the original two members—Luke and Grant. Grant began to joke about masterminding a school shooting. The joke soon turned serious when Luke discovered a list of students Grant wanted dead. In September, Grant was adamant about turning the idea into a reality. He made elaborate plans that ultimately involved Luke physically carrying out the scheme.

Luke recalled, "I had a feeling that everything was coming to an end for me, and I just wanted it to happen. I was tired of living." Days before the actual shooting, Grant approached Luke and ordered him to kill his mother, retrieve the gun from her closet, take it to school, and kill Christina and whoever was in his path before the police apprehended him. Luke was in tears and begged his leader not to make him do it. Grant responded by comforting him one minute and the next minute threatening him if he didn't carry out the murders. Grant reminded Luke of all the years he had been tormented by bullies and treated unfairly by his mother, Christina, and society in general. He also encouraged Luke by telling him he would be famous—he would be glorified for his actions, and songs would be written in his honor.

Luke was a basket case for four days. His mind swirled with conflicting thoughts and the consequences from carrying out or not carrying out the crime. During this time he retreated in silence. He stayed home from school and spoke to no one. On Tuesday, September 30, 1997, Grant called and told him tomorrow was the day. There were no excuses or reasons to prevent Luke from committing murder. The shootings would happen, and that was final. Grant's persuasiveness finally overrode Luke's fear.

The following day, October 1, Luke grabbed a butcher knife and, after a few practice stabs on his bed, walked into his mother's bedroom. Overwhelmed by confusion and frozen by fear, he stood paralyzed. He began numbly repeating a mental mantra that he was good for nothing and would always be good for nothing. When his mother opened her eyes, Luke began stabbing her to death. "I don't know how many times I stabbed her . . . I just really can't remember any of it after that moment." Luke doesn't remember any more details of his mother's murder, but vaguely recalls Grant calling to congratulate him. The police report includes that he had beaten her with a baseball bat, breaking her upper and lower jaw. He then wiped down the blood-marked walls and washed his jeans.

After he snatched the rifle his father had left behind, Luke hopped in his car and drove to school. He went inside the building with a collection of songs and poems he had written and handed them to one of his friends. Grant had promised to publish them for him, after Luke's imminent death.

He then returned to his car, hid the .30-30 rifle under his blue trench coat, and walked in the front doors of the school at roughly eight o'clock in the morning. As he walked into the school, he yelled, "This ends now!"

"I went into the school and shot Christina, and then I turned and shot Lydia Dew. I really didn't mean to shoot Lydia specifically; I just turned and pulled the trigger. At that point, I felt something leave me. I think it was probably most of the demons. I didn't know what to do, so I just started walking around and firing."

Luke's massacre left three people dead—his mother, Christina, and Lydia—and wounded seven other students. Amid the screams, the blood, and the pandemonium, Luke walked out of the school, got into his car, and started driving away. He didn't know that the assistant principal, Joel Myrick, who was armed with a handgun, was following him. After Luke slammed his car into a tree, Joel ordered the bewildered teen out and held him at gunpoint until the police arrived. Luke said that had he driven farther away from the school grounds, he would have committed suicide: "All I really wanted to do was get my life over with."

In his taped confession Luke said, "I didn't want to kill my mother, I do love my mother. I just wanted revenge on Christina and my mother." As Luke sat in jail that afternoon, a detective visited him in his cell. He informed Luke that he had spoken with Grant, who had told police that Luke made a pact with Satan to kill Christina. He blamed Luke for everything and feigned innocence and shock at what had happened. At that moment, Luke realized he had been lied to and used. His loyalty, devotion, and trust in Grant meant nothing. He was just a mindless pawn in a fatal game, easy prey for manipulation. This broke Luke's heart. All he had wanted was to be accepted. And after he thought he finally was, he had destroyed his own life as well as the lives of innocent people.

During the ten-month period between his involvement with the Kroth and the murder, a drastic and violent internal change took place. Luke wrote, "All I can really say is that from my own decisions, Grant's manipulation and brainwashing, and demonic possession, I went from being a school nerd to a cold-blooded killer who was completely devoted to Satan and my leader [Grant]." This type of negative transformation takes place in many teen killers for different reasons we will explore.

CAUSE #1: AN ABUSIVE HOME LIFE AND BULLYING

Killers often come from abusive homes, some worse than others. While this is a subjective term and can characterize many situations from enduring physical or sexual abuse from parents, living with a mentally ill mother or father, or being in a home environment dominated by alcoholism or domestic violence, these situations are breeding grounds for a future violent child. Any major disruption in a home—such as constant moving or relocating to an entirely new country—can also have a significantly negative impact on a child. Events and situations like these can prove highly emotional and problematic to an adolescent.

The family unit has changed drastically in the last few decades. Today, for instance, something as simple as eating dinner together as a family has become a rarity. According to the U.S. Census Bureau, only 55 percent of fathers eat dinner with their kids every day. Mike Huckabee, author of *Kids Who Kill,* recorded that more than 80 percent of all violent juvenile offenders are products of broken homes. He also said that nearly 70 percent live in single-parent homes, and nearly 90 percent of these violent teens have suffered some sort of physical, sexual, or emotional abuse.

Clay Shrout, from Union, Kentucky, killed his parents and two younger sisters, then proceeded to take a class hostage at his high school.

On May 26, 1994, seventeen-year-old Clay Shrout from Union, Kentucky, killed his parents and two younger sisters and took a class hostage at his high school. He had recently gotten into trouble for bringing a stun gun to school and was mad at his parents because they had taken his weapons away. Clay was heavily into violent music, horror movies, and pornography, and he dabbled in the occult.

When I met with him, he told me his anger stemmed from his mother sexually abusing him as a child. We continued corresponding after our initial meeting. Clay wrote:

When I was an infant, my mother began to sexually molest me . . . she was supposed to be giving me baths. Soon the molesting stopped, and I blocked all the memories and fear and rage remained for years after . . . Because of my fear, I enjoyed violence. It was my shield . . . I grew to love violence . . . I would spend hours thinking about hurting/killing people. I would also spend time thinking about raping/sexually abusing women.

Clay said he understands that the sexual molestation did not "make" him kill and that essentially he "chose to be violent."

Clay continued, "I took one of my dad's guns, and killed my father, mother, and two sisters. I killed my mother because I hated her. I killed my father first, because I was scared that he would hurt me for killing his wife. Then I killed my sisters so that they wouldn't have to live alone and in misery—"

I have dedicated chapter 5 to the dilemma of bullying, as I believe it is a huge contributor to teen violence. Practically every school shooter in America was bullied to some degree at school. On the day of the Columbine massacre, school shooter Eric Harris wrote in his journal, "By now it's over. If you are reading this, my mission is complete . . . Your children who have ridiculed me, who have chosen not to accept me, who have treated me like I am not worth their time are dead." Fellow killer Dylan Klebold recorded his own thoughts in a video a few hours before the shooting: "I'm going to kill you all. You've been giving us s—t for years."

CAUSE #2: VIOLENT ENTERTAINMENT AND PORNOGRAPHY

I'm a firm believer that violent entertainment and pornography do much more damage to teens than many people are ready to admit. Our teens are bombarded with violent and obscene imagery from a very young age. The primary mediums that feed our kids this garbage are the Internet, television, video games, movies, and music. Many children and teens have full access to these modes of entertainment, and I believe this can reap very dangerous consequences. Chapter 4 details the connection between violent entertainment and real-life violence.

Pornography is a major problem. How popular and successful is the pornography industry? According to Dr. Jerry R. Kirk in his book *The Mind Polluters,* the industry currently has higher sales figures than the fast-food chain McDonald's. Governor Mike Huckabee, in his book *Kids Who Kill,* states that pornography has become the fastest-growing segment of the American entertainment industry. In my opinion, excessive exposure to pornography fuels sex crimes that, particularly for a teen, can turn into a sexual murder. Many teen killers who rape and kill are either into or have been exposed to pornography. Numerous serial killers have acknowledged the connection between pornography and murder. In chapter 4 you can find an excerpt from serial killer Ted Bundy's last interview before his execution, in which he explores this topic.

Tim Erickson from Minnesota was inspired to start a vampire cult after watching the movie The Lost Boys. *On a camping trip, Erickson egged on a group of friends to help him kill a fellow camper and drink his blood. They beat the man to death and cut his throat.*

With a connection to a 1987 movie about teen vampires, *The Lost Boys,* Timothy Erickson, eighteen, and several codefendants committed a murder in Minnesota known as the "Vampire Murder of St. Cloud." Before the crime, which occurred on March 21, 1988, Timothy had watched the film and was inspired to form a vampire cult. On the day of the murder, he and a bunch of guys, including the murder victim, Donald Gall, went camping. The group huddled around a fire at a campsite later that night and talked, laughed, drank, and smoked marijuana.

After Donald fell asleep, Timothy and three friends went into the woods, where Timothy suggested they kill Donald and drink his blood. While some balked at the plan and refused to participate, Timothy was intent on carrying it out. They returned to the campfire, and Timothy initiated the murder by clubbing Donald over the head with a tree branch while two others kicked him. After the victim lost consciousness, Timothy and an accomplice pulled out a knife, grabbed the victim by his hair, and slit his throat. They also stabbed him in the heart and slit his wrist. As Donald lay bleeding to death, Timothy allegedly licked the blood off of the knife and pushed the victim's body into the icy river. The killers were soon arrested and are serving lengthy sentences in the Minnesota corrections system.

CAUSE #3: ANGER, DEPRESSION, AND SUICIDE

It may seem obvious that quite a few teen killers suffer from anger problems as well as clinical depression. Many of them are suicidal, and in today's violent culture, when violent teens choose to end their lives, they purposefully do it with great drama. They go out in a blaze of glory, like in a video game, taking as many people down with them as possible. If the killer survives, he or she often feels tremendous guilt, and most say they wish they had never committed the crime. But by then it's too late. There must be a better way to address troubled teens' internal havoc and prevent them from resorting to murder.

Depression is a major problem for many Americans. Most adults who suffer from it treat it like any other disease and take medication or seek counseling. Many parents, unfortunately, prematurely assume a teen's depression is just typical teenage angst rather than consider it a genuine cause for concern. Some kids who don't have an outlet to deal with their torment deeply internalize their depression until one day their emotions erupt and irreparable damage is done.

According to William Pollack, a Harvard University psychologist, depression and suicide are contributing factors to school shootings. He explained, "By the time of the shootings, a good 78 percent of the perpetrators were suicidal."[2]

Teen suicide has increased 200 percent since 1960.[3] Recent statistics suggest that one teenager commits suicide every two hours.[4] I understand this can be quite a frightening topic, especially for parents. Yet we must address and deal with it so young people can be given hope instead of being ignored.

William "Scott" Lang killed the only person who probably cared about him, his former girlfriend's father. He broke into his girlfriend's house and shot her father to death as he returned home. He contemplated killing his ex-girlfriend and her mother, but instead fled the scene.

William "Scott" Lang, from Clearwater, Florida, broke into his ex-girlfriend's house and murdered her father on December 21, 2001. When Scott was three, his biological mother put him up for adoption, and soon after he was adopted into the Lang family. After being thrown out of his adoptive home because of his unruliness, he bounced around to a few families from his church. Eventually he found himself homeless and without family. He told me:

I ran out of money . . . I was homeless, depressed, broke, and felt there was nothing left for me to do, and nowhere to turn. I set my mind to end my life, but the horrible person that I am decided to inflict pain on other people to show them what I felt like. I am truly ashamed of what I did, I wasn't at the time, I didn't care what people thought or would say about the horrible thing I was about to do.

Lang continued:

I went to his [Richard, the father of his ex-girlfriend, Katie] house while everyone was at work . . . I got the gun and waited. At that point I wasn't sure if I wanted to kill Katie, kill them all, or just make them watch me kill myself . . . He [Richard] came in and was greeted by me and a gun . . . I told him I was going to make Katie watch me blow my brains out. At this, he stood up and said I was going to have to make a choice, kill him or he was leaving . . . he wasn't going to let Katie come home. As he turned around and walked to the front door, I shot him . . . I killed the person who was probably the most active in trying to help me, and took away the father and husband of people who loved me . . . I sat in their house with Richard dead and waited again for Katie to come home. Katie came home and was shocked and scared. I held her at gunpoint for an hour . . . I told her to take her clothes off. I was going to rape her. Then her mother came home.

William then stole their family car and took off, and was arrested soon after. His sentence was life in prison.

CAUSE #4: DRUG AND ALCOHOL ABUSE

Chapter 3 addresses this subject, so I won't take much time exploring it here. One of the most interesting stories I have come across, however, that illustrates the connection between substance abuse and murder is Paula Cooper's case. Paula's poisons were alcohol and marijuana.

In May 1987, fifteen-year-old Paula Cooper and three of her friends cut school and drank alcohol and smoked marijuana. They planned to leave their home state of Indiana and schemed of committing a robbery so they could get their hands on a vehicle and some money. The group went to the home of one of Paula's neighbors, seventy-eight-year-old Ruth Pelke, a Bible teacher. The victim let them into her home when they told her they wanted to learn about the Bible. When Ruth went to get her Bible, they attacked her. In tears Ruth began to recite the Lord's Prayer. Paula then grabbed a large butcher knife and stabbed the elderly victim more than thirty times. The wounds were fatal.

The group was eventually caught joyriding in the victim's vehicle. Paula was convicted and given a death sentence. Her sentence created such an uproar that even Pope John Paul II spoke out against it. Eventually her sentence was reduced to sixty years in an Indiana prison. The other accomplices were given sentences of twenty-five to sixty years. With good time earned, Paula could be released as early as 2014.

CAUSE #5: CULTS AND GANGS

Although there are some differences between cults and gangs, the basis of their objectives is similar—to promote and engage in violent activity in the name of a specific cause or group.

These packs include skinhead sects, street gangs, and hate groups. More and more young kids are being recruited into gangs to commit violent crimes because, if caught, the punishment is less severe for an underage juvenile. Children are being initiated into gangs as young as ten years old!

In 1993 in T. C. Jester Park in Houston, Texas, six members of the Black and White gang—eighteen-year-olds Derrick Sean O'Brien, Jose Medellin, and Peter Cantu; seventeen-year-olds Efrian Perez and Raul Villarreal; and fourteen-year-old Vernancio Medellin—were initiating a young man into their gang. Their priorities quickly shifted when they lustily eyed two teenage girls walking nearby. The girls were taking a shortcut through the park to get home before their curfew.

The gang members grabbed one of the girls while the other tried to escape. Apparently feeling tremendous guilt, the fleeing young lady turned back and went to help her friend. For more than one hour, both of them were gang-raped and beaten, then strangled to death.

O'Brien and Cantu have been executed. Jose Medellin is still waiting for his execution date, and Vernancio, the juvenile, was sentenced to forty years in prison. The others are serving life sentences.

Cause #6: Easy Access to and Fascination with Weapons

What do you think is the easiest thing to blame when a school shooting occurs? You guessed it—guns! As I've studied teen crime, I've observed that teens using guns have committed a significant number of murders. But for every teen murder that involves a gun, there are at least one or more murders where a gun is not the weapon of choice. Chapter 6 will detail this subject more thoroughly.

I'm torn as I approach this controversial topic. On the one hand, guns are very dangerous and should be kept out of the hands of teenagers. Knowing this, I want to do my part to educate the public about how to lock up guns, where to safely store them, and how to keep them out of the hands of our children. On the other hand, I believe carrying a legal, licensed concealed weapon is a safety precaution that can benefit and help keep society safe. So the questions I keep asking and answering are: *Can guns be bad? Yes.*

Can guns be good? Sure. Will we ever get the guns out of the hands of the bad guys? No. Can we try to do our best to keep guns out of the hands of children and troubled teenagers? Definitely.

Oregon school shooter Kip Kinkel was given his own gun after a psycho-therapist suggested that Kip's dad purchase one for Kip so they could have an activity to participate in together. Kip was not only stockpiling guns in his bedroom, but his parents were even buying them for him.

In 1998, Kip killed his parents and shot many innocent students at his high school with the gun they bought him. As you read the chapter on guns, my hope is that you can see how dangerous guns can be and also learn about their positive aspects—how they can also save lives.

CAUSE #7: PEER PRESSURE

Peer pressure is an age-old plague that predominantly affects young people and can be quite an influential factor in committing crimes. Some teens are only "along for the ride" when a crime is committed and end up suffering the same punishment as the person who actually committed the crime. Peer pressure guides other teens into situations in which they feel there is no way out. And there are others who become enmeshed in a crime because they are simply at the wrong place at the wrong time.

Sam Archer, along with two friends, robbed a convenience store in Des Moines, Iowa, and in the process killed the store clerk. Archer didn't swing the hammer that killed the clerk but helped grab money from the cash register.

In Des Moines, Iowa, on March 24, 1990, three teens, part of "the Young and the Wasted" gang—ringleader Phillip Negrete, nineteen; Jammi Reimer, fifteen; and Sam Archer, fifteen—were partying together. Late that night they decided to steal some beer at a local store. In the process of the robbery, the store clerk was killed. Phillip struck the victim in the back of the head with a hammer, instantly killing him. Jammi and Sam then stole sixty-one dollars from the register, and the three young men fled the scene.

In my communications with Sam, he gave me some pretty revealing and frightening insights into peer pressure: "Ever since I was old enough to understand everything that was going on around me, I always was trying to be a part of everything, especially if it was something mischievous."

Sam told me that he looked up to his brothers and sisters, who were terrible role models. They were regular abusers of drugs and had been incarcerated several times. "They let me smoke pot with them and drink as well. But I wanted to do what seemed to excite them even more. I wanted to steal things from people and stores . . . I began doing that around the age of eight or nine." Sam was frequently in and out of juvenile detention centers from a very young age because of the robberies, burglaries, and acts of vandalism he had pulled off.

Perhaps the crime is best expressed in his own words:

> The night that the murder took place, we were all at a party—Jammi, Phil, and myself. It was about three in the morning when we ran out of beer, so Phil and I decided to go steal from a convenience store. We talked to a couple of people about going with us and Jammi was the one who agreed to go. My best friend at the time, Jesse, said no and he was usually the one who did everything with me regardless of whether it was legal or illegal. He actually made a statement to me that said, "Please don't go, brother, because I feel like something bad is going to happen. That is why I am not going." But, needless to say, I did not listen.

He is positive he would not have been involved in the murder if he would have "just stayed in school" or been in his "parents' house sleeping that night getting rested for school the next day."

CAUSE #8: POVERTY AND CRIMINAL LIFESTYLE

POVERTY

Children who grow up in a community marked by poverty are at risk for futures laden with violence. Statistically, poverty is a breeding ground for criminal activity, drug use, unstable families, illiteracy, and a whole host of other problems. Poverty doesn't always have to mean devastation for families and children. There are plenty of people who have overcome destitution and lead productive, successful, and positive lives. Yet there is an undeniable pattern, and many children raised in poverty do take up a life of crime.

What alarms me is that many of these young people end up in prison in disproportionate numbers. Quite frankly, I am sick and tired of meeting men in prison who had a very small chance of having a crime-free future because of their upbringing in poverty-ridden communities. I am desperate to do something about this tragedy. As a nation we need to focus more attention on our internal situation, on our own country. We need to invest in our neighborhoods, cities, and states and give young people who are impoverished a chance to thrive.

William Garner grew up in Cincinnati, Ohio, in a poor, abusive, and unstable home. He described his home to me as a "dysfunctional environment with violence, injury, physical and sexual abuse, and abject terror." In the absence of parents or respective guardian care, William and his siblings were left to fend for themselves. He explained that they were so poor they were "deprived of proper food and nourishment, having to exist at times upon 'sugar' bread." William started committing robberies and burglaries to get money for food. During this time of crisis, William was also molested and abused by family members and family friends.

William did a short stint in prison at the age of eighteen, and when he was nineteen, he was arrested, convicted, and placed on death row for the following crime.

William Garner in prison. He set a house on fire after a robbery, killing five children.

About three in the morning on January 26, 1992, William walked into a hospital to get a sandwich in the cafeteria. He saw an unattended purse lying on a counter, grabbed it, and took it into a restroom. After pilfering through the handbag and finding nothing of value inside, he called a cab to take him to the address of the person who owned the purse. William broke into the home and stole a TV and a VCR.

Before leaving, he set a fire in hopes that the smoke alarm would go off and wake the kids who were home at the time. He also said he hoped the police would come and remove the children from the home when they saw the terrible living conditions. The fire ended up engulfing the residence and killing all five children.

Police believed that William set the fire on purpose to eliminate the witnesses, but he pleaded with me to believe that he did not intend to hurt the children. He was given a death sentence and is now waiting for his execution date.

CRIMINAL LIFESTYLE

When I talk about criminal lifestyle as a contributing factor, I am referring to murder committed during another crime. Many teen killers murder their victims during, for example, an armed robbery or a burglary of a victim's home.

Wesley Shafer was robbing a convenience store with another young man in South Carolina when he reflexively shot the clerk right between the eyes. Wesley stood about six feet away from the victim. He claimed the shooting was a mistake and that he was only planning on robbing the store to get money to buy drugs. Wesley also mentioned the influence of the movie *Menace to Society.*

CAUSE #9: LACK OF SPIRITUAL GUIDANCE AND APPROPRIATE DISCIPLINE

LACK OF SPIRITUAL GUIDANCE

I have met many inmates who have gotten in touch with their spirituality and have completely turned their lives around for the better. Many of them believe that if they had received spiritual guidance earlier, chances are they would not have committed their crimes and would not be locked up today. I correspond with many inmates who have had a spiritual awakening and seem to be truly rehabilitated. This list includes many inmates with whom the general public is unfamiliar, but also includes notorious names like

David "Son of Sam" Berkowitz, Charles "Tex" Watson from the Manson Family, and school shooter Luke Woodham.

This topic doesn't sit well with a lot of people, especially the ones who would refer to this internal shift as "jailhouse religion." I've heard many folks sarcastically ask, "Well, who wouldn't turn to God after being locked up?" I can assure you that many offenders who are locked up do not turn to God or spirituality but instead continue their violent behavior in prison.

Ben Darras, who committed a murder in 1995 that has been connected to the movie *Natural Born Killers,* is an example of a rehabilitated person. After watching the film—globally recognized for its horrific and constant display of glorified violence—Ben departed on a cross-country crime spree with his girlfriend. He killed an adult male victim and paralyzed an adult female victim.

Today Ben is not the same violent person as he was when he was arrested. He is active in the religion program at the Mississippi State Prison and attends a seminary program there. I was not only impressed with the change in Ben's life but also by the life-altering program made available at this prison. Classes and textbooks are available to the inmates as well as opportunities for corporate worship, prayer, and fellowship. This allows them to make incredible changes and become better people. I am convinced this is the only way we will see true change among violent offenders.

Ben spoke to me about the importance of spirituality and right upbringing. He related that as a young person, he lacked direction, discipline, and accountability. He feels those are the reasons he started down the wrong path, which eventually led to the death of one person and the permanent paralysis of another. He said, "When I was eighteen, I was living life totally out of control and made one horrible mistake after another . . . After my arrest I had a lot . . . of time to reflect on my life. I came to some conclusions about myself. I realized that I had absolutely nothing to be proud of in my life. Even worse, I didn't know if my life had any meaning or purpose at all."

LACK OF APPROPRIATE DISCIPLINE

Another common issue for teen killers, besides the lack of spiritual guidance, is the absence of appropriate discipline in their homes. Many teenagers today have absolutely no discipline in their lives, and so not only do whatever they deem fit but even dominate their households and their schools. Parents and teachers seem to be afraid of these kids, and sometimes rightly so. When I was in school as a kid, I remember being disciplined for causing trouble, and then would get it even worse when I returned home. I grew up in a Catholic elementary school, and the teachers would smack my knuckles with a ruler; in middle school the principal even paddled me. Once I got home, oh boy, did the wrath of my father ever straighten me out!

While I am not advocating these specific forms of punishment, I can assure you that these techniques did wonders to curb my delinquent behavior. I firmly believe many kids today have no concept of discipline at home or at school. It is unfortunate that many times when parents try to appropriately administer discipline, they are either reported to child services or greeted by a visitor from the local police department. This new approach to discipline will one day come back to bite us big time. I stand behind Proverbs 13:24: "He who spares the rod hates his son, but he who loves him is careful to discipline him."

CAUSE #10: MENTAL ILLNESS AND BRAIN INJURIES

Although some people may assume that most murderers suffer from mental illness, it's certainly not always the case. Most teen killers are technically sane, but there are some who do suffer from legitimate mental illness. Mental illness and brain injuries can consist of overactivity in certain parts of the brain, indentions of the cranium, documented neurological abnormalities, and head injuries.

What saddens me is the large number of mentally ill teenagers who are locked up in maximum security prisons alongside the rest of the inmate population. The days of mental institutions are long gone, and there are prosecutors who seem to believe that the best way to rehabilitate violent offenders who suffer from mental illness is to shove them in prisons with everyone else.

Kevin Hughes is one of the many teen killers I regularly correspond with. On March 1, 1979, when he was sixteen years old, Kevin killed a nine-year-old girl in Philadelphia, Pennsylvania. She was found raped and strangled. He was not caught, and he struck again one year later—sexually and physically assaulting another young girl. Kevin confessed to the crimes and told police that "voices" made him kill. While being held for trial, mental health professionals at the prison and professionals at a psychiatric hospital noted the severity of his mental problems. Still, two doctors somehow found Kevin competent to stand trial. A third doctor, however, conversely suggested Kevin was "profoundly disturbed." Before the trial—the concept of which he did not understand—Kevin believed all he had to do was tell his story to the judge and he would then be allowed to go home.

Kevin's home life was extremely unstable. His mother was a diagnosed schizophrenic, an alcoholic, and a drug abuser. On many occasions she had sex with men in front of her children. Kevin was also sexually abused by at least one man, who told him that men should forcibly subdue women.

Kevin sends me many letters, but I can't decipher what he is trying to say. His writings are unintelligible; I can only read and understand every third or fourth word. It definitely disturbs me that Kevin is in a prison and not in a mental institution where he could be receiving help to stabilize his mind.

THE TOP THREE REASONS WHY TEENS KILL

There are many more reasons why teens kill, but the ones I listed above are the most common. If I were to narrow it down to the top three reasons, the order would be as follows:

1. Abusive families and bullying
2. Violent entertainment and pornography
3. Anger, depression, and suicide

Kids who grow up in an unstable home are more likely than other children to develop violent tendencies. Violent entertainment, which fascinates many teenagers, significantly contributes to teens violently acting out in reality what they see on TV, watch in a video game, or listen to in a rap or death metal song.

And finally, teenagers who are depressed and suicidal could be pushed to act on their feelings to end their lives. Their act of suicide many times begins with homicide. Many of today's teen killers were initially suicidal, but decided to "take other people with them." Teenagers today are raised in a culture of death, and murder seems to be something that comes naturally as a way to solve their problems. Something drastic needs to be done to take the violence out of our everyday culture.

FOR MORE INFORMATION ON TEEN MURDER AND THE CASES COVERED IN THIS BOOK, LOG ON TO WWW.PHILCHALMERS.COM. DON'T MISS PHIL'S BOOK, *THE ENCYCLOPEDIA OF TEEN KILLERS.*

THREE

PREMEDICATED MURDER: THE SUBSTANCE ABUSE CONNECTION

I was a kid affected by depression and hopelessness, that drug combination [referencing his alcohol and cocaine addiction] only intensified what I was already going through . . . my life would have turned out differently if I didn't ever start.

—EUGENE TURLEY,
teen killer, as told to author

Luke Woodham was not high on drugs or alcohol when he committed his crimes. He also never experimented with the two substances Eugene Turley was addicted to. So while Luke's story might seem irrelevant to this chapter, he definitely has some strong opinions about the correlation between drug and alcohol abuse and violent behavior.

Prison life is full of "if onlys." *If only* I'd never picked up that gun. *If only* I'd not acted in anger. *If only* I'd left the pipe alone. *If only* I wasn't drunk that night. These are the statements that echo throughout the prison halls—the words of failed lives. I've been hearing them for ten years and I know them all too well. Sadly, a lot of them are connected to drug and alcohol abuse.

These guys all believe that their lives would have been completely different for them if they wouldn't have started using drugs and abusing alcohol. A lot of people make terrible mistakes because of the impairment their drug addiction causes on their minds. After hearing all of the stories I've heard in prison for the last ten years, it seems like 90 percent of violent criminals were addicted to or using drugs and alcohol while they committed their crime. It is best stated in the Greek word for witchcraft, *pharmakeia*, where we get our word *pharmacy*. In biblical days occultists would take drugs to open their minds to evil spirits. Should we think any differently today?

Teens don't kill; it's the drugs that make them kill. This is one of the most common statements I hear from both parents and kids, though it is not entirely true. For every teen who killed while using drugs, I can present you with another who was either not a drug user or was sober at the time of his or her crime. As I've mentioned before, there is no one direct cause that makes a teenager kill; many contributing factors are involved. Still, drug use is a major concern and one of the leading causes of teen violence and murder.

One study showed that 85 percent of violent teens claimed to be habitual users of marijuana, and 55 percent used other illegal drugs.[1] I know there are hundreds and thousands of teenagers who abuse drugs or alcohol and do not become teen killers. When substance abuse is coupled with underlying issues like clinical depression, sexual abuse, or even severe bullying, however, there is a greater chance a teen will become violent, even to the point of committing murder. Quite frankly, it becomes much easier to do almost anything when one is intoxicated and one's judgment is significantly impaired.

Beverly Eakman, author of several internationally acclaimed texts on education policy, commented, "The basic things these drugs do is they steal the will. By stealing the will, I mean they destroy your inhibitions, so that any inhibition that you had not to do certain things, you just don't have it anymore—including getting angry."[2]

There are generally three effects drugs or alcohol have on a teen killer. The first and most obvious is the harmful, mind-altering effect of a drug; the second is the buildup of violent and destructive emotions that results from withdrawal from a drug; and the third is the power of addiction that incites teens to murder or commit other violent crimes in order to feed their deadly habit. One of these three motivations typically drives drug-influenced teen killers.

Drug use has been around practically forever. As a matter of fact, it appears five times in the New Testament. The Greek word for drugs, as Luke earlier referenced, is *pharmakia*. In *Vine's Expository Dictionary of New Testament Words, pharmakes* refers to "a sorcerer, especially one who uses drugs, potions, spells, enchantments."[3] Back then almost no one used drugs except for witches and sorcerers. They were mainly used in pagan worship rituals to hallucinate and to communicate with evil spirits.

Revelation 18:23 says, "By your magic spell [*pharmakia*, or drugs] all the nations were led astray." When examining modern-day teen drug use, we cannot discredit the early connection and uses for drugs in ancient civilizations. It should be no surprise that when young people use illegal, harmful, and mind-altering drugs, they carry out crimes that seem evil or even satanic.

According to streetdrugs.org, the top ten misused drugs in the world include tobacco, alcohol, prescription drugs, methamphetamine, marijuana, ecstasy, crack cocaine, heroin, steroids, and inhalants. While the number of drugs I could discuss in this chapter is almost endless, I will focus on only a handful of the most popular ones associated with violent crime.

METHAMPHETAMINE

In my opinion, the number one drug that poses the greatest threat to our society is methamphetamine, also known as meth or crystal meth. Meth is a highly addictive and powerful stimulant that affects the central nervous system. It causes mood swings, anxiety, euphoria, depression, delusional thinking, paranoia, and even permanent psychological damage. Prolonged use of meth can cause damage to the heart, liver, kidneys, and lungs, which can ultimately lead to death.

Meth—sold in powder, ice, and tablet forms—can contain dangerous ingredients, including battery acid, drain cleaner, lantern fuel, and antifreeze. According to the 2005 National Survey on Drug Use and Health (NSDUH), an estimated 10.4 million Americans ages twelve or older had used methamphetamine at least once in their lifetimes for nonmedical reasons.[4] Another recent survey indicated that 2.7 percent of eighth graders, 3.2 percent of tenth graders, and 4.4 percent of twelfth graders reported lifetime use of meth.[5]

On January 22, 2003, meth users and siblings Beau Maestas, nineteen, and Monique Maestas, sixteen, from Mesquite, Nevada, attacked and stabbed two children. One child was three years old, and the sibling was ten years old. Beau and Monique used butcher knives to slash their victims after they woke them up from a peaceful sleep. The three-year-old died from the injuries; the other was paralyzed.[6]

Before the murders, the victims' mother had sold Beau and Monique salt instead of meth. Enraged, the two decided to take revenge and killed the dealer's children. The Maestas siblings grew up in an abusive home, and their parents were addicted to meth. It was also reported that their father had given Beau some advice on how to get even with someone who wrongs you—kill their family! The father is also currently serving a prison sentence for murder.

PRESCRIPTION AND PSYCHIATRIC DRUGS

According to streetdrugs.org, prescription narcotic drugs are some of the most used and abused medicines—whether they are illegally obtained or prescribed to the user. Prescription drugs can be classified into three categories: narcotics (including Oxycontin, Vicodin, and Percocet), depressants (including Xanax, Valium, and Librium), and stimulants (including Ritalin, Dexedrine, and Meridia). Drugs like Ritalin can lead a user to experience feelings of hostility and paranoia. Higher doses of a drug like Xanax can cause impairment of judgment and irritability as well as paranoia, suicidal thoughts, agitation, and aggressiveness.

In 2007, the Partnership for a Drug-Free America reported that nearly one in five teens abused prescription medications to get high the previous year.[7] A 2006 report published by the NSDUH stated that prescription drugs are the most commonly abused drugs among twelve- to thirteen-year-olds. According to the 2006 "Monitoring the Future Study" by the University of Michigan, Vicodin, cough syrup, and tranquilizers/sedatives are part of the top five drugs used by high school seniors.

We must also consider the dangers of drugs that are prescribed to teenagers today, including the much publicized and popularized Ritalin. In September 2002, a congressional hearing held by the House Government Reform Committee convened to investigate the documented overdiagnosing and overmedicating of mental disorders in children. Committee chairman Rep. Dan Burton alleged that approximately 6 million kids in America were taking the psychiatric drug Ritalin—the drug that the DEA places in the same category as opium, morphine, and cocaine.

I do believe that Ritalin may be beneficial in treating hyperactivity or other disorders in young people. It seems, however, that many physicians are simply in the habit of writing out prescriptions for this drug without performing comprehensive examinations on the patient or investigating alternative solutions. Ritalin poses potential danger, and doctors need to prescribe this drug using utmost caution.

Dr. Peter Breggin, one of the foremost experts on the dangers of prescription drugs, wrote that Ritalin and other stimulants "do not 'normalize' the brain; they render it abnormal. This cannot be over-emphasized: Stimulants produce pathological malfunctions in the child's brain. Whenever these drugs have any direct effect on the child's mind or behavior, they do so by disrupting brain function. In short, effective doses of Ritalin always cause malfunctions in the brain."[8] Even the manufacturer of the drug warned that "frank psychotic episodes can occur" with abusive use.

There are also some potential dangers in the effects of withdrawal from psychiatric drugs like Ritalin. In 1995, Denmark's Cooperative Institute for Medical Drug Dependence communicated that symptoms of withdrawal from psychotropic drug dependence included "emotional changes, fear, terror, panic, fear of insanity, irritability, aggression, an urge to destroy, and an urge to kill."[9] Additionally, the American Psychiatric Association's *Diagnostic and Statistical Manual of Mental Disorders* lists one of the major complications of Ritalin withdrawal as suicide.

There are many crimes connected to prescription drugs—whether prescribed to the violent offender or used for nonmedical purposes. In 1986, fourteen-year-old Rod Matthews beat a classmate to death in Massachusetts. He lured his victim into the woods near his home and repeatedly hit him with a baseball bat. Known as a gifted student, Rod had been taking Ritalin and Methylphenidate since he was nine years old. Weeks before, he had told a teacher that he had an urge to kill somebody. The teacher's response? She replied that murder was a felony. That's all she said.

Rod's family disclosed that after he had been on these drugs, his demeanor completely changed. Once known as the class clown, Rod became unusually quiet, withdrawn, and calculating. He reached out for help another time when he placed a note in the "problem box" at his school. The note read, "My problem is I like to do crazy things. I've been lighting fires all over the place . . . lately I've been wanting to kill people I hate, and I've been wanting to light houses on fire. What should I do?" After Rod was arrested, he was taken off the psychiatric drugs, and his violent behavior stopped.

In an interview with *Freedom Magazine,* Dr. Fred Baughman, a pediatric neurologist, commented on the case.

> He [Rod] began to have very disturbing, violent thoughts about killing and things like this. I have come to believe that violent, angry thoughts are commonplace with amphetamines and they can intrude acutely, that is, within days of starting the drug. So I hear stories all the time, "This child was never an angry child, never an aggressive child, until the Ritalin" or "until the Adderall" or what have you. And it can be right away or it can be after a lag period.[10]

We can't ignore desperate teens' cries for help. And we certainly can't just tell them to pop more pills. We need to be sure we are doing everything in our power—as parents, teachers, and even politicians—to appropriately nurture and foster the mental health of our children. We must intervene with good common sense when a young person's mental state appears to be compromised and thoroughly research all possible solutions to remedy their health.

Fifteen-year-old Kenny Bartley, from Jacksboro, Tennessee, opened fire at Campbell County Comprehensive High School on November 8, 2005. Kenny killed an assistant principal and seriously wounded the principal and another assistant principal. The boy had been sent to the principal's office because of rumors that he was carrying a gun. When school administrators saw the weapon and tried to wrestle the gun away from him, Kenny started shooting. Court testimony revealed Kenny's addiction to drugs, and he stated he had taken two Xanax pills immediately before the shooting. Kenny said that the crime would not have occurred if he had not taken the pills. He also told investigators that he stole his father's gun and brought it to school to trade it for the drug Oxycontin.

Scott Turnland, from Alabama, started experimenting with pot and alcohol when he was twelve years old. A year later his habit evolved into hardcore stuff, and he started using crack, opium, and acid. When he was fourteen years old, after engaging in frequent domestic disturbances and getting in trouble at school, he was ordered by the state courts to see a psychologist, who diagnosed him with bipolar disorder (manic-depressive illness). The doctor suggested that a psychiatrist treat Scott to medicate him for his illness.

Scott began taking psychotropic drugs in small doses. After his psychiatrist increased his dosages, his behavior worsened. He became more depressed, and antidepressants were then added on top of the other drugs. At the age of fifteen, his condition was so bad his parents sent him to another psychiatrist, who said Scott was taking way too many prescriptive drugs and began to slowly wean him off the pills. In the meantime, this new doctor placed him on Neurontin, which he referred to as a new, highly effective medication. Scott wrote me and said that "two days after he placed me on that new medication I wigged out and killed my brother for no reason."

Two months after Scott was sentenced, the FDA black-labeled (provided a warning on the prescription box) Neurontin because of the extreme negative side effects it had on patients, including hostility, stress, depression, suicidal tendencies, and violence. Apparently the drug had never been approved to treat mental illness and was only supposed to be used for patients suffering from epilepsy, shingles, and nerve disorders.

CRACK AND COCAINE

Cocaine is the most potent stimulant of natural origin. The powdered, hydrochloride salt form of cocaine can be snorted or dissolved in water and injected. Crack—a highly addictive drug that has gained tremendous popularity in recent years—is cocaine that has not been neutralized by an acid to make the hydrochloride salt. This form of cocaine comes in a rock crystal that can be heated and its vapors smoked.

The high obtained from either drug can last between five and thirty minutes. Once the drug leaves the brain, the user experiences what's called a "coke crash" that can lead to depression, irritability, and fatigue. Crack or cocaine users continually place themselves in danger of having strokes or heart attacks, which could result in sudden death. Other dangers include seizures, cardiac arrest, and respiratory arrest. Long-term effects can include aggressive paranoid behavior combined with depression.

Seventeen-year-old crack user and teen killer Leslie Torres went on a seven-day crime spree across New York in January 1988. He robbed multiple people, killed five, and wounded six others while high on crack cocaine. Convicted of first degree murder, Leslie was given a sentence of sixty years to life in prison.

On December 6, 1998, in Fairfax, Virginia, sixteen-year-old Eugene Turley shot and killed a thirty-year-old mother of four over a seventy-five-dollar cocaine debt. Eugene, who was molested as a child, was also a fan of violent movies like *Scarface* and *The Godfather*. He regularly abused drugs and alcohol and was under the influence when he committed the crime.

Eugene communicated to me that he was "intoxicated on both alcohol and cocaine during the commission of [his] crime." He also explained, "I was a kid affected by depression and hopelessness; that drug combination only intensified what I was already going through . . . my life would have turned out differently if I didn't ever start using drugs—I would have never committed murder."

Eugene described his addiction: "You become a slave to the drugs, and there is a huge black cloud in front of your eyes, and you can't see anything except that next hit or drink." He was convicted of murder and sentenced to life in prison.

PCP

PCP is a drug that can have dangerous and deadly results. Developed in the 1950s as an IV anesthetic, this drug was never officially approved because of the intensely negative psychological effects produced during clinical studies. Users of PCP can become very violent and suicidal and many times possess an enormous amount of strength. For example, some users have been able to fend off several police officers at the same time. This drug can be snorted, smoked, or taken orally. According to the National Institute on Drug Abuse (NIDA), 2.4 percent of high school seniors have reported using PCP at least once.[11]

Brenda Spencer, whom I introduced in chapter 1 of this book as the first known female school shooter, was an admitted PCP user. She shot and killed two people and wounded ten others in 1979.

LSD

LSD, also known as acid, is another dangerous drug that can cause severe psychological effects. It is one of the strongest mood-altering drugs on the market and is sold as capsules, tablets, liquid, or absorbent paper. A person taking LSD can experience severe delusions and visual hallucinations.

(Left photo) Jason Lewis in between his sister and nephew and (right photo) in his prison photo. Jason shot and killed his parents while they watched television.

Fifteen-year-old Jason Edward Lewis shot his parents on March 5, 1995, in Newman, Georgia. Jason began using drugs like speed, alcohol, marijuana, and particularly LSD, when his sister moved out of the family home.

Suffering from low self-esteem, Jason believed he would start getting more attention from his parents since his sister was gone, but the attention shifted instead onto his mentally ill mother. Troubled and confused, he turned to drugs as an escape.

Jason initially thought about running away, but was later persuaded by his friend Kevin to kill his parents instead. Jason recounted the crime to me:

> I set the phone down in the kitchen, and Mom and Dad can't see me. They're watching TV. I shot them two times each . . . I looked down and the shotgun had swung up into my mouth as I was pumping it and pulling the trigger . . . I was trying to kill myself but there were only four shells. There was supposed to be five shells.

Jason said, "I felt like I was standing in the corner watching myself doing it. Even now, when I think about it, my memories are of me looking at myself from behind, watching myself do it."

He said he wouldn't have killed if he had not been under the influence of drugs, and painfully told me, "I'm still dealing with what I've done. It's something that will haunt me forever. That's something I must accept."

ALCOHOL AND MARIJUANA

While many people label alcohol and marijuana as harmless substances, they are anything but! On April 12, 1985, fifteen-year-old Ronald Ward killed two elderly women and a twelve-year-old boy in West Memphis, Arkansas. Ronald stabbed them repeatedly with a butcher knife. One of the women may have been raped. He initially pled not guilty to his crime but has recently admitted his guilt. Ronald explained to me that he committed his crime because of the destructive combination of negative peer pressure and heavy drug and alcohol abuse. He was sentenced to death at the age of fifteen, making him the youngest person on death row in the United States at that time. Though his sentence was later commuted to life without parole, he died from cancer in prison at the age of thirty-eight.

On May 25, 1987, fifteen-year-old Andrea Williams and her seventeen-year-old boyfriend, Mario Garcia, killed Andrea's mother in New York. Using a hatchet and a knife, the couple violently stabbed her because she threatened to end their relationship. Investigators said that Andrea and Mario were high on drugs at the time of their crime. Andrea habitually smoked marijuana. Both were convicted of murder, but Williams has since been released from prison. Garcia will probably be released soon as well.

INHALANTS

Most people don't think about inhalants as part of the drug problem, but because they are available in practically every home in America, a significant number of teens are abusing these products. The 2005 Partnership Attitude Tracking Study (PATS) recorded that one in five teenagers (20 percent), or 4.7 million teenagers, nationally abuse inhalants in their lifetime. Another study showed that 4.5 percent of high school seniors used inhalants during the last month. Users of inhalants sniff the vapors from chemicals found in common household products—nail polish, insecticides, kerosene, air-conditioning fluid, cleaning solvents, aerosol whipped cream, and propane—or pour them on a rag and breathe them in through their mouths. A new trend called "dusting" involves inhaling computer cleaners that dust off computer keypads. Several deaths have been attributed to dusting. Inhalant users can suffer from damage to vital organs and the central nervous system. Depression, heart failure, asphyxiation, and aspiration can also occur when used in high doses.

WHAT CAN BE DONE?

Is there a solution to this troubling drug epidemic among American youth? Can we get our kids off drugs and keep children from experimenting with them? While I definitely don't have all the answers, I do have a few ideas.

DOCTORS: PRESCRIBE APPROPRIATE MEDICATION

School shooter Kip Kinkel from Springfield, Oregon, shot and killed his parents, then opened fire on his classmates on May 21, 1998. By the end of the day, two people were dead and twenty-two were injured as the result of his violent rampage.

Kip reportedly had taken Prozac and Ritalin before he acted out in rage. The statements he made before the crime and during interviews with the investigators immediately after the murders are truly revelations into the mind of not only a teen killer but of a medicated teen killer. Kip explained to police, "Oh, my God, my parents were good people, I'm just so f—ed up in the head." He exhibited obvious psychiatric problems when he exclaimed, "G— d— . . . these voices inside my head."[12] Was Kip mentally ill, or is there a possibility that the psychiatric drugs he was taking made him snap?

As laypeople we need to work with the medical community to effectively address the negative effects that may result from taking certain medications. We need to evaluate whether or not certain prescribed drugs are the best way to rehabilitate or treat teens with mental or emotional issues. What other options might be available to better serve our teenagers who need help?

We also need more research on the prescription drugs for hyperactivity and ADHD that many physicians are giving our kids like candy. In my younger days, when I saw a child who was rebellious or hyperactive, I also usually saw a parent who was quick to apply discipline and make the child understand the necessity of behaving. There were no doctors who would quickly diagnose a mental disorder—instead of what simply might be a discipline issue—and prescribe a popular drug. I believe that many of the drugs out there that were created to suppress or cure hyperactivity can cause our kids to become depressed and even violent. Doctors should closely and regularly monitor the teenagers who are on these medications to ensure that the results are positive and not negative.

Not only that, but I know there are many parents out there who need a wake-up call! Whatever happened to good, old-fashioned discipline? Withholding rewards when children disobey? Not letting them run the household? Monitoring what they do? It's sad that many parents and even youth leaders, such as teachers or counselors, are afraid to punish teenagers when they do wrong. Instead, they attribute their actions to a mental or emotional deficiency and let their behavior slide, or shove a pill in their mouths to hopefully calm them down. Shame on us!

GOVERNMENT: SUPPORT DRUG TREATMENT FACILITIES

When a teenager is convicted of a drug charge, I believe there should be mandatory sentencing to a drug treatment facility. Unfortunately, they are very expensive. We say in America that we are fighting the war on drugs, but are we really? I speak to parents every week across the country who are trying to get their kids help for their drug problems, and there are not that many places to turn. Because most drug-treatment facilities are outrageously expensive, most parents cannot afford them and, therefore, drug-addicted teens are not getting the treatment they need.

The United States government needs to step up and help. If we are really going to effectively fight the war on drugs, we need to establish drug treatment facilities operated by the government and paid for with American tax dollars. We can either pay for minors to get drug treatment or keep locking them up and paying for their incarceration for many, many years to come. What are we willing to pay for? Six months in rehab or fifty years in prison?

If you are a parent of a drug-addicted teen, I believe your best solution is to send your teen to a drug treatment facility. I know the cost is overwhelming, but it's the best option at this time. The NIDA proposed that "scientific research since the mid-1970s shows that drug abuse treatment can help many drug abusing offenders change their attitudes, beliefs, and behaviors towards drug abuse, avoid relapse, and successfully remove themselves from a life of substance abuse and crime."[13]

Researchers at the NIDA estimated that for every dollar spent on addiction treatment programs, there is a four- to seven-dollar reduction in the cost of drug-related crimes. Sadly, in a 2004 NSDUH study, it was recorded that while 22.5 million Americans age twelve and older needed treatment for substance abuse and addiction, only 3.8 million people received help. Only 17 percent of Americans are getting the treatment they need for substance abuse. This is not good enough! We need to do more to promote the effectiveness of drug treatment facilities, lower the costs for American families, and make sure our teenagers get help.

LAWMAKERS: START GETTING TOUGHER

Another solution in helping to diminish our country's drug crisis is to start enforcing tougher drug laws and stiffer sentences. The tremendous cost of untreated substance abuse to our communities includes violent crimes, property crimes, prison expenses, court costs, criminal costs, emergency room visits, child abuse, child neglect, lost child support, foster care, welfare costs, reduced productivity, and unemployment.[14] The NIDA suggested that successful drug abuse treatment in the criminal justice system can not only help reduce crime but stop the spread of HIV/AIDS, hepatitis, and other infectious diseases.[15]

What's the bottom line? We need to keep our kids off drugs. Whether you are a parent, a teacher, a youth leader, a police officer, or a guidance counselor, you can help eradicate this nationwide plight. Talk to kids openly about the dangers of drug use. Educate them about the horrible realities of addiction. Encourage them to participate in extracurricular activities, whether sports or volunteer events, that develop and strengthen their self-esteem and confidence. Do whatever you can to keep the growing monsters of drugs and alcohol away from kids. Let's build a safer and stronger community together.

For more information on helping loved ones beat drug and alcohol abuse, check out the helpful Web sites in the resource section at the back of this book.

FOR MORE INFORMATION ON TEEN MURDER
AND THE CASES COVERED IN THIS BOOK,
LOG ON TO WWW.PHILCHALMERS.COM.
DON'T MISS PHIL'S BOOK,
THE ENCYCLOPEDIA OF TEEN KILLERS.

FOUR

ENTERTAINED TO DEATH: VIOLENT ENTERTAINMENT

The media is the catalyst that pushes them [teen killers] over the edge.

—GREGG MCCRARY,
former FBI criminal profiler,
commenting on CNN's *Burden of Proof*

Luke Woodham's primary influence in life became occult worship, but violent entertainment also played a significant role. Music provided a delusional source of sanity. Horror movies fed his violent cravings. Role-playing video games offered him an escape from reality. Luke can't pinpoint one specific movie, band, or video game that birthed his violent streak. It was the constant exposure to these things that caused him to be apathetic about others and life in general. He wrote me a lengthy letter on the psychological impact violent entertainment had on him.

> Throughout all of my entertainment choices, one thing remained the same—my entertainment started off innocent and simple but grew darker and darker as time lapsed. As my entertainment choices changed, I changed along with them. I strongly believe that these were conduits which my personality changed through. Also, I was rejected more and more because of these personality changes, so I sought consolation for my rejection in the same things, mainly music. It is a trap! The more these things changed me, the more I was drawn into them.

I think that all of the death, violence, cussing and sex that is fed to our children (and adults) through the media has a very negative effect on people. Not only do I think that it desensitizes people, but it can give them ideas, inspiration and motivation to be able to do things that they normally wouldn't or couldn't do. I've seen countless times here in prison where people would rap songs about killing and violence just to build up the courage to harm another person. They had to psyche themselves up on rap to get the "b—ls" to do something they couldn't on their own.

An abundance of violence in entertainment is never a good thing. While I don't believe that violent entertainment by itself is responsible for creating teen killers, I am convinced that it can act as a goad for turning today's rebellious and troubled kids into tomorrow's violent criminals. As Gregg McCrary, a former FBI criminal profiler, commented on CNN's *Burden of Proof*, "The media is the catalyst that pushes them [teen killers] over the edge."

There are hundreds, perhaps thousands, of examples I could use to illustrate the disgusting amount of violence that inundates the entertainment world, but I will only focus on a couple of them and related crime incidences. If you'd like to dig a little deeper into what kinds of movies, music, and video games are marketed to our children, please refer to the list at the back of this book.

Be aware that there is a lot of foul language and disgusting content in the examples you'll read in this chapter—and that is only what my publisher allowed me to leave in. Believe me, this is mild compared to what your kids are actually exposed to.

VIOLENCE ON THE BIG SCREEN

Although violent entertainment can be imaged through a variety of modes, movies provide perhaps the greatest impact because of the surround-sound audio effects and the life-size images projected on the big screen. Luke told me that Grant Boyette, the leader of the satanic cult he was involved with, regularly quoted lines from violent movies and imitated the behaviors and actions of the bad characters because he thought "they were cool."

Here are a few movies that have sparked some major controversy.

THE MATRIX

Directed by Andy and Larry Wachowski and released in 1999, this film is the first entry in a series of *Matrix* movies, video games, and comics. The movie describes a future world of simulated reality. While *The Matrix* has spiritual undertones, its violence is overwhelming. People are run over by trains, decapitated, shot, impaled, and so on.

On February 17, 2003, Josh Cooke, nineteen, from Oakton, Virginia, was eating dinner with his parents on a typical Monday night. Later that evening, as he was listening to the song "Bodies" by the metal band Drowning Pool, he glanced over at his *Matrix* poster above his bed and then looked longingly at his gun. Josh put on his combat boots and a black jacket, similar in appearance to the character Neo in the movie. He filled his pockets with ammunition and walked out of his bedroom, 12-gauge shotgun in hand. Minutes later, he shot and killed both of his parents in the basement. After calmly dialing 911, Josh waited for the police to arrive.

Josh told me, "I woke up late in the morning feeling pretty normal and helped my father shovel our driveway and then the neighbor's driveway. Afterwards, I literally stayed in all day watching television and playing violent video games like *Grand Theft Auto* and *Blood Rayne*, and watching *The Matrix* movie on VHS, my new copy." Josh told me that after he killed his parents, he "then grabbed a coke out of the refrigerator and drank it while I waited for police to arrive and arrest me."

"Matrix *killer*" *Josh Cooke, who shot his parents to death in the basement of their home while listening to Drowning Pool's song on his headset. The song contains the lyrics "Let the bodies hit the floor."*

Not only did he regularly play violent video games more than six hours a day, but Josh watched *The Matrix* so many times he actually wore out the video. He said, "I was very connected to *The Matrix* because I really identified with it, and I still do today. Every time I watched it, I imagined the people Neo was killing were my enemies. It felt almost therapeutic and it was a lot of fun."

Transaction # 19/269
Register # 19
Initials _____

GALYAN'S
SPORTS & OUTDOOR ADVENTURE

Gun Deal Sheet № 283924

Date 2 / 15 / 03
Name COOKE, JOSHUA, PAUL
Street 10504 ADEL ROAD
City OAKTON State VA Zip 22124
Phone (703) 281-2543
County of Residence FAIRFAX

DESCRIPTION	RETAIL	
Make: REMINGTON	419	99
Model: MODEL 870 ESM		
Serial #: C599529A		
Barrel Length: 20" / 26"		
Gauge/Caliber: 12 GA		
ID Type VA DL		
ID #: T66O7-6642		
FF		
SF K684349	Paid in	
CHK 06434E	full	
UPC 047700257141		

NOTICE TO BUYER

• WE ARE NOT RESPONSIBLE FOR MAINTAINING ANY OF YOUR PERSONAL GUN RECORDS FOR YOU. PLEASE KEEP YOUR COPY OF THIS INVOICE FOR YOUR FUTURE REFERENCE.
• ALL FIREARMS AND AMMUNITION SALES ARE FINAL AND NO REFUNDS OR EXCHANGES ARE PERMITTED. ANY DEFECTIVE NEW FIREARM UNDER WARRANTY WILL BE RETURNED TO THE MANUFACTURER FOR REPAIR OR REPLACED AT THE MANUFACTURER'S DISCRETION. USED GUNS ARE WARRANTED FOR 7 DAYS ONLY TO FEED, FIRE AND EJECT.

Sold by: _____ 16053

Customer Signature: _____

Receipt from the purchase of a shotgun by Josh Cooke, which he used to gun down his parents in the basement of their home. Josh was inspired by the movie The Matrix.

Josh described the murder: "So many things were building up . . . this thing just happened, I just exploded like a time bomb."[1] He told me he believed that he committed the crime because of his rage and insanity. "I was abused my whole life by family," Josh said to me. "My adoptive mother beat my sister and I with belts and other objects, and when we wet our beds she would press and hold our faces into the urine on the bed and call us vile names."

Just before murdering his mom and dad, Josh had downloaded information from the Internet about the Washington, D.C., sniper attacks in 2002, and read how Lee Boyd Malvo, one of the two snipers, was also obsessed with *The Matrix*. The attacks that occurred in and around Virginia, Baltimore, and Washington, D.C., left ten people dead and critically injured three. After Lee was arrested, he yelled from his jail cell, "Free yourself from the Matrix" and told the FBI agents that they should watch *The Matrix* if they wanted to understand him. Jailers found lines of dialogue from the movie scribbled on paper in his cell.

MENACE II SOCIETY

This 1993 film features violence in inner-city Los Angeles and is permeated with rampant drug use, carjackings, and drive-by shootings.

On January 23, 1994, Caryon Johnson, thirteen; Kunta Sims, seventeen; and sixteen-year-olds Steven Johnson, Sylvester Berry, and Calvin Smith shot and killed James Pearson in Lone Oak, Kentucky. The media referenced the event as a "*Menace II Society* murder." These individuals kidnapped their victim at gunpoint, drove him around in his car, and then Kunta shot him to death. The man's body was dumped on the lawn of a random house. The next day the dangerous group shot and injured another young man, Matthew Fiorentini. They are all currently serving lengthy prison sentences for their violent crimes.

Another group of young men under the age of twenty who were obsessed with *Menace II Society*—Sean Sword, Patrick Weatherwax, Gregorio Riojas, and Eugene Pickard Jr.—shot and killed a retail clerk in Michigan on March 16, 1994. After they robbed the store, the group struck again ten hours later and knocked off a florist and a pizzeria. Detective Doug Hummel of the

Oakland County Sheriff's Department said that these young men had watched the film several times and were acting out parts of it.

NATURAL BORN KILLERS

In this movie two young people—Mickey (Woody Harrelson) and Mallory (Juliette Lewis)—fall in love, engage in a bloody killing spree in public places like convenience stores and restaurants, and gain fame as a result. The film garnered international attention because of its excessively graphic and violent content. Director Oliver Stone stated in a *New York Times* article on April 14, 1996, "The most pacifistic people in the world said they came out of this movie and wanted to kill somebody."

To date, the most deadly school shooting in America by a teen was influenced by *Natural Born Killers*. Eric Harris and Dylan Klebold killed thirteen people and wounded twenty-four others on April 20, 1999, in Littleton, Colorado. The two disturbed teens were fascinated with Nazi beliefs, weapons, and pipe bombs, and were heavily involved in violent video games such as *Doom* and music like KMFDM. They watched *Natural Born Killers* more than fifty times and even named their killing spree in its honor—"the holy April morning of NBK [Natural Born Killers]."

In a journal entry, Dylan wrote, "I'm stuck in humanity. Maybe going NBK with Eric is the way to break free . . . I hope we kill 250—"[2]

In his journal, Eric wrote, "NBK. I love it! Sometime in April, me and V [Dylan] will get revenge and kick natural selection up a few notches—"[3]

SCARFACE

Written by Oliver Stone and starring the legendary actor Al Pacino, this 1983 movie depicts the tumultuous journey of a vicious Cuban drug lord, Tony Montana. Stone garnered many of his ideas from extensive research into real crimes while consulting with the

Prison photo of New York teen killer Austin Addison, who shot and killed another male teen in the process of stealing his "starter" jacket. He took great pleasure in seeing and starting fires.

Miami police and the DEA. The film was so violent that the Motion Picture Association of America originally rated it "X" for its extreme violence and obscenity. Director Brian DePalma was able to get the MPAA to furnish an "R" rating right before the film's release. He admitted, however, that the content didn't change much from its original condition.

On November 21, 1986, eighteen-year-old Austin Addison shot and killed Hillary Spruell in Mount Vernon, New York. Why? Because Hillary refused to give up his jacket. When I asked Austin about his relationship with violent entertainment, he answered, "I enjoyed movies like *Scarface* and any other movie that depicted sex, drugs, and violence. And yes, movies did play a role in what I did and the way I committed my crime. We all want to be Tony Montana in *Scarface*."

THE NEW PORNOGRAPHY: GORE PORN

I recently read an article written by film journalist and television personality Johanna Schneller. She remarked on the alarming amount of violence being portrayed in horror films and categorized them as "gore porn." To qualify as gore porn, Schneller said "a scene must take something that's already disgusting . . . then amp it up for maximum nausea-inducement . . . and the whole thing must be accompanied by repetitive thrash music."[4]

Luke Woodham's obsession with horror movies, or gore porn, began at the mere age of four. As a young boy, he secretly watched these flicks and grew to love the feeling of terror he experienced when he witnessed its main characters slash and hack innocent victims. But that feeling of fear gradually transferred to sheer excitement. On-screen torture and mutilation gave him a sick sense of pleasure. Instead of gasping at bloody scenes, he laughed. According to Luke, grotesque murder scenes, like the ones depicted in the following movies, have thrilled many fellow teen killers and school shooters.

THE SAW SERIES

Lionsgate released this movie series complete with nonstop, elaborate gore porn. Victims at the mercy of a psychopathic genius known only as "Jigsaw" are given the opportunity to unravel a puzzle of their fate. They are handed weapons and clues to help them along their way. A character in *Saw III* performs a pretty gory operation on Jigsaw. She pulls back his scalp with a pair of pliers and uses a drill to cut a hole in his skull. She then handles a power saw to cut a piece out of his skull.

The Associated Press reported that after screening this film, France's culture minister Renaud Donnedieu de Vabres decided to ban minors from seeing the movie because of its "violence and intolerable, incessant sadism." Clearly, it fulfilled the objective of producer Darren Lynn Bosman to "disturb and disgust."[5] If only everyone would have the courage to protect children as Prime Minister de Vabres did!

SCREAM

Another illustration of gore porn is the slasher movie series *Scream,* directed by Wes Craven and produced by Miramax Films. This series grossed more than $161 million worldwide. Unfortunately, this makes the case for creating profitable entertainment that glamorizes violence and lacks any semblance of morality and decency.

This tongue-in-cheek horror series revolves around a killer known as "Ghostface." The main character wears a Halloween mask reminiscent of the *Scream* painting by Edvard Munch and spends his time murdering innocent people. A disgusting abundance of murder, bloodshed, and sexual activity saturates each movie.

According to Wes Craven, "Kids today have very real and generational-specific fears and they need a way to process these terrors in a positive and funny manner."[6] Exactly how does Craven define "positive and funny manner"? By stalking, shooting, blowing up, brutally stabbing, and bludgeoning his movie characters.

One of the film's stars, Neve Campbell, was so disturbed that she told talk-show host Rosie O'Donnell she refused to watch her own work.[7] I think that says it all when a main character in a movie can't even watch the film she acted in!

On May 10, 1998, Jessica Holtmeyer, sixteen, and her friend Aaron Straw, nineteen, from Clearfield, Pennsylvania, hung fifteen-year-old Kimberly Dotts from a tree and then beat and killed her with a large rock. During their trial, a witness testified that after Jessica watched *Scream* she said, "It would be fun to hang somebody" and that after the murder took place she acknowledged, "I'd like to do it again."[8] Jessica allegedly also wanted to keep one of the victim's fingers as a souvenir.

(AP Photo / Keith Srakocic)

Jessica Holtmeyer, sixteen, is led out of the Clearfield County court by sheriff's deputies after testimony in her trial in Clearfield, Pennsylvania, on January 26, 1999. She was convicted on January 28, 1999, of hanging a learning-disabled teenager.

Seventeen-year-old Mario Padilla and his sixteen-year-old cousin Samuel Ramirez killed Mario's mother, Gina, July 1999 in Los Angeles, California. Mario stabbed his mother to death as Samuel held her down. In a taped confession to police, the boys said they killed and robbed Gina to get enough money to buy costumes like the one used by the killer in *Scream*. They also informed police they intended to wear those costumes when they killed several of their classmates. Thankfully, they were captured before they could carry out that crime.

THE TEXAS CHAINSAW MASSACRE

Another popular example of gore porn is New Line Cinema's remake series of *The Texas Chainsaw Massacre*.

Reviewer and journalist Steven Isaac, of pluggedinonline.com, called the movie "a sadistic pornography of violence gruesome beyond proper description. It celebrates death. It glorifies brutality . . . It's squalid, wretched, debased, debauched, depraved, abhorrent, contemptible, loathsome, repulsive, revolting and repugnant."

(AP Photo / Bob Child)

Todd Rizzo, eighteen, being led into court for the killing of a thirteen-year-old neighborhood kid with a sledgehammer because he wanted to find out what it felt like to kill someone. He was motivated by the movie The Texas Chainsaw Massacre and idolized serial killer Jeffrey Dahmer.

Todd Rizzo, age eighteen, from Waterbury, Massachusetts, murdered a thirteen-year-old boy on September 29, 1997. Todd idolized serial killers, and *The Texas Chainsaw Massacre* was his all-time favorite flick. Todd lured his victim to a wooded area behind his home with the promise of looking for snakes. Then Todd smashed the boy in the back of his head with a sledgehammer, the same weapon used by the insane family in the movie.

When describing his obsession with this movie, Todd said, "I've seen the disturbing series probably as many times as I've seen my own reflection in a mirror. I imagined myself part of that insane family—" He was convicted of first degree murder and sentenced to life with no parole.

SEX AND VIOLENCE: A MATCH MADE IN MOVIE HEAVEN

In many movies I consistently see the marriage of gratuitous violence and sexual imagery. In talking with hundreds of teen and adult serial killers, this combination provocatively appeals to those who have tendencies toward violence.

Radio personality and best-selling author Dr. James Dobson interviewed Ted Bundy, one of America's most infamous serial killers, shortly before Bundy's execution in 1989. Bundy had many strong opinions and spoke adamantly against the coupling of violence and sex in entertainment. He also made the definite connection between violent and sexualized entertainment and real-life crime. Bundy explained:

> The wedding of those two forces, as I know only too well, brings about behavior that is just . . . too terrible to describe. There is loose . . . people like me today, whose dangerous impulses are being fueled, day in and day out,

by violence in the media . . . particularly sexualized violence . . . I tell you there are lots of other kids playing in streets around this country today who are going to be dead tomorrow . . . because other young people are reading the kinds of things and seeing the kinds of things that are available in the media today.

VIOLENT MUSIC:
SHOCK ROCK, DEATH METAL,
GANGSTA RAP, AND HORRORCORE

When his internal world became too much to handle, Luke Woodham's CD player and headphones became his "saving grace." Bands like Nine Inch Nails, White Zombie, Rancid, and Cyprus Hill continually blared in his ears. Artist Marilyn Manson wrote Luke's favorite songs—"The Man You Should Fear" and "Tourniquet." He felt his life paralleled the themes of Manson's album *Antichrist Superstar* and Nine Inch Nails' *The Downward Spiral*.

When Luke got his first Walkman CD player, he became obsessed with music. It was his life. Subsequently, his grades began to drop and his urges to isolate increased. Not knowing what else to do, Luke's mother confiscated his personal radio. His addiction to music became apparent at that time as he sank into an even deeper depression and became physically ill. It seemed as if he was going through withdrawal.

Luke was ruled by the influence of music. It controlled his emotions. If he felt happy, he would listen to a sad song and immediately digress into misery. When he listened to violent songs, the thrashing beat and repulsive lyrics would fuel a desire to become violent. He wanted to punch someone. Destroy something. Even kill.

Listening to rap music changed his vocabulary for the worst. Women became "b—s" and "sluts" and almost every other word out of his mouth was an obscenity. At the time he was only eleven. When Luke graduated to hard rock and shock rock music, though his vocabulary improved, his emotional and mental state became more morbid. Thoughts revolving around death and destruction saturated his impressionable teenage mind.

Many of Luke's fellow inmates share his same opinions about the influence of violent music. They have told him that they committed their crimes after listening to songs that psyched them up and gave them the "guts" they needed to follow through with the kill.

The American Psychological Association backed up this theory. They released a study in 2003 on the effects of violent lyrics. The study found that college students who listened to violent songs were more likely to engage in aggressive behavior and have angry thoughts. Lead researcher Craig Anderson, a professor at Iowa State University, was not surprised by the findings, but strongly urged parents to recognize this grave issue and act accordingly. He indicated that parents should have a say in what their children listen to at home. Additionally, the American Academy of Pediatrics affirmed that popular music can contribute to depression, suicide, and homicide.[9] The American Medical Association also concluded that music with destructive themes could be harmful to some teenagers.[10]

Many music producers, record companies, and artists behind the creation of violent music deny moral responsibility for their art and hide behind words like *free speech, warning labels,* and *parental responsibility.* Yet the music they manufacture and distribute celebrates rape, sodomy, violence, murder, and obscenity; and they gear most of their marketing efforts toward children, teenagers, and young adults.

Jamie Rouse, a school shooter who killed three people in November 1995, claimed violent music impacted him. He told me, "I'm not blaming the music for what I did. I'm just saying that it was a factor . . . Inspired by this music I chose to adopt these beliefs . . . I joined one of those music clubs and discovered death metal music. This music made me feel evil and powerful, even capable of murder. It was almost a high."

It matters what your children are listening to! It matters what kind of lyrics their favorite artists are singing! While not all music is bad, of course, there are a number of musicians who seem to use artistic leverage to endorse a message of violence and destruction.

SHOCK ROCK AND DEATH METAL

Cannibal Corpse. Formed in 1988, the death metal band Cannibal Corpse established a cult following after the release of their early 1990s albums, including *Butchered at Birth* and *Tomb of the Mutilated*. While these titles already establish a gruesome tone, here is a sampling of some of their lyrics: "The sledge my tool to torture . . . pounds down on your forehead—"

In Eugene, Oregon, on April 10, 1994, four friends—Daniel Rabago, sixteen; Michael Hayward, nineteen; Jason Brumwell, eighteen; and Johl Brock, nineteen—met at Jason's house to mastermind a robbery. They needed cash to buy marijuana, so they schemed to loot a local grocery store. During their planning session, this group listened to death metal music, including Cannibal Corpse. Daniel later testified, "We were all into evil and we were all pretty much 'deathers.'" He described "deathers" as people who have "a lot of hate in them and sees the morbid things in life."

At eleven that night, they entered the store and demanded that the clerk, Mrs. Ream, hand over the money in the cash register. When they noticed a second clerk stocking shelves in the back, they grabbed her and repeatedly pummeled the back of her head with a metal rod, shattering her skull. Michael finished the job.

As the getaway car was being prepared, they led petrified Mrs. Ream to the back of the store and brutally beat and stabbed her. The group fled the scene when they heard some noises and, fortunately, were arrested four months later trying to cash stolen lottery tickets. They were all found guilty and imprisoned.

Mrs. Ream amazingly survived the attack but lost half of her blood, a large portion of her scalp, and suffered several broken bones. She sustained permanent damage to her arms and hands.

Daniel explained that the crime was committed to honor members of Cannibal Corpse.

Marilyn Manson. Marilyn Manson garnered commercial success in the 1990s from his controversial appearance, music, and performances. Holder of the title "Reverend" in Anton LaVey's Church of Satan, he also called himself the "Antichrist Superstar."

Marilyn Manson's real name is Brian Warner, and he attended a Christian school in Canton, Ohio. Unrelentingly picked on for years, he strongly identifies with teenagers who suffer from abuse and are considered social rejects. Marilyn uses his frustration and hatred of authority and mainstream society to fuel his passion to write music. Music with lyrics like "I bash myself to sleep . . . I slit my teenage wrist."

School shooter Kip Kinkel was an avid listener to Marilyn Manson's music. The fifteen-year-old killed two students and injured twenty-five others in Springfield, Oregon. Just before his murderous rampage at the high school on May 21, 1998, this Marilyn Manson–obsessed kid shot his parents to death.

Slipknot. This nine-piece musical group from Des Moines, Iowa, was formed in 1995. Ironically, these musicians claim they care about children because, after all, they are parents themselves. I question their moral codes when I read their alarming statements about their young fans. One band member said, "There are guys out there who would pick their eyes out with a f— coat hanger and go, 'Aaargh!' They're for you . . . And little kids are really into it too . . . Get them young, like the tobacco companies say!"[11]

Does it really sound as if they care about kids?

Two Slipknot fans killed a young man on April 24, 2003, in San Bernardino, California. Sixteen-year-old Amber Rose Riley and twenty-year-old Jason Lamar Harris convinced their victim to walk with them to a nearby park. There they stabbed the poor man more than twenty times and cut his throat. The pair admitted to listening to the song "Disasterpiece" before and after the kill. The lyrics declare an undeniable sentiment of murder: "I wanna slit your throat . . . and feel the swoon." Amber told investigators she also had watched the movie *Satan's School for Girls* shortly before the crime. Both killers were convicted of murder and sentenced to prison.

GANGSTA' RAP

Eminem / D12. In today's teen music market, we can't discuss rap without talking about superstar Eminem, a white rapper from Detroit whose real name is Marshall Mathers. Eminem has incredible talent, but it's unfortunate that he uses his talent to destroy, poison, and pollute this generation of young people. He makes a living with obscene and violent rants about rape and murder in his lyrics such as "This girl's only fifteen . . . cut this b—'s head off—"

Eminem eventually shifted his solo career to include his group into his stardom and named the group D12. In the song "These Drugs," the group raps, "Missin' since yesterday, perfect just for rape." "Just Like U" includes, "Rapin' an . . . smoke crack, smack a b—."

Eminem's protégé, 50 Cent, also raps a message of violence and murder with lyrics containing lines like "I'll ride by and blow ya brains out."

Tupac. Tupac Amaru Shakur, otherwise known as 2Pac or Tupac, was recognized in the *Guinness Book of World Records* as the best-selling hip-hop artist. More than seventy-five million of his albums have been sold worldwide. He was a rich man who lived the high thug life, was the target of many legal battles, and was gunned down and killed at the young age of thirty-six. He died in the same destructive manner he portrayed in his artistry. Tupac's lyrics include "No faces for open caskets, peelin' yo cap backwards."

In Texas, on April 11, 1992, nineteen-year-old Ronald Ray Howard shot and killed a Texas state trooper during a routine traffic stop. Ronald said he had been listening to Tupac's album *2Pacalypse Now*. He was an avid fan of violent rap music, and his legal team even proposed that violent music motivated him to commit his crime. Other fans of Tupac include the Jonesboro, Arkansas, school shooters Andrew Golden and Mitchell Johnson, two of possibly the youngest school shooters ever.

Many rap artists celebrate violence and murder in their music. The Ying Yang Twins rap, "I feel like shootin' fool . . . I'll f— around and kill you." Method Man and Redman brag about killing in the song "Blackout": "Date-raper with juvenile eighth graders, slicin' jugulars." Rapper Nas wrote about a murder-suicide with his girlfriend: "One between the eye, she's died . . . put the nine to my head, pulled the trigger."

Nathan McCall, an African-American writer trying to get the attention of the rap industry, poignantly commented, "This negative message of destruction and denigration of life has got to stop . . . It is having a corrosive effect on young black Americans who hold these rappers up as heroes. Their songs are overwhelming the power of parents, teachers, and other figures of authority."[12]

In the wake of radio host Don Imus's controversy (Imus made racist remarks about a college women's basketball team while he was on the air), Jason Whitlock, an African-American columnist for the *Kansas City Star*, made the following statement in an issue dated April 11, 2007:

> Thank You Don Imus. You've given us [black people] an excuse to avoid the real problem . . . While we're fixated on a bad joke cracked by an irrelevant, bad shock jock, I'm sure at least one of the marvelous young women on the Rutgers basketball team is somewhere snapping her fingers to the beat of 50 Cent's or Snoop Dogg's or Young Jeezy's latest ode to glorifying nappy-headed pimps and hos . . . At this time we are our own worst enemies. We have allowed our youths to buy into a culture [hip-hop] that has been per- verted, corrupted and overtaken by the prison culture. The music, attitude, and behavior expressed in this culture is anti-black, anti-education, demean- ing, self-destructive, pro-drug dealing and violent.

HORRORCORE

Insane Clown Posse. Another violent rap group with a loyal following is the horrorcore/hip-hop/rapcore duo Insane Clown Posse, or ICP, consisting of Violent J (Joseph Bruce) and Shaggy 2 Dope (Joseph Utsler). They almost always wear black and white face paint to resemble evil clowns.

ICP raps perverse lyrics such as "I like to murder, leave a mother f—'s throat hanging open—"

Although in my opinion this group isn't particularly loaded with talent, they know how to appeal to kids who feel like outsiders. These kids believe ICP provides a safe community where they can interact with and relate to one another. In my travels to prisons across the United States, I have met many ICP fans who are locked up for violent crimes, including murder.

Two fans of this group, sixteen-year-old Sarah Kolb and seventeen-year-old Cory Gregory of Illinois, killed a classmate and dismembered her body on January 21, 2005. Sarah was jealous over the victim's instant popularity as the new girl at school and wanted to do something about it. They beat and strangled sixteen-year-old Adrianne Reynolds in a Taco Bell parking lot. Sarah and Cory panicked after they realized the victim was dead, so they took the body to Sarah's grandmother's farm. There they burned Adrianne's body, dismembered it with a saw, and dumped the body parts at a state park and at the farm.

Sarah's profile on an ICP Web site included the words "gouging your eyes out with a f— spork."

Horrorcore rap music fan Jeff Weise, sixteen, shot and killed nine people and injured fifteen others before killing himself at the Red Lake High School in Minnesota on March 21, 2005. Jeff kept a journal filled with dark and depressing writings and drawings. He was a fan of Twiztid, a group who toured with ICP and boasted about their obsession with serial-killer horror films. Jeff also loved to listen to Mars, a rap-metal artist who is also affiliated with ICP. Mars's latest album is called *Some Girls Deserve to Die*. Jeff was said to be obsessed with a song titled "Go Suicidal" that included "Just put that pistol to your chin." On MTV's Web site—a liberal media channel—Mars's music is described as "drenched in bloody, violent images."

Jeff's fixation with Mars's music was so publicized that the controversial story reached Mars himself. In an interview after the shooting, the rapper defended himself by saying, "I write a lot of crazy lyrics, but there's something wrong about anyone who blurs the line between reality and entertainment. Maybe it inspired him [Jeff], but no one knows what was going on in Jeff Weise's mind."[13]

Mars admitted that kids obsessed with suicide, murder, and guns regularly visited his Web site, but he refused to be held accountable for any part in fueling a young person's violent rage. "My responsibility as an artist is not to change my lyrics to something soft and poppy. What about teachers, principals, and parents? They had some responsibility, and they're the ones who could have saved this kid."[14]

Does that sound right? Blame everyone else. Blame the parents. Blame the teachers. Just don't take moral responsibility for any of your own actions.

TELEVISION: BYE-BYE BRADY BUNCH

Of all the violent media available to children and teens, television is probably the most accessible. It's also the hardest for parents to monitor. Although there is technology that protects children from violent imagery, most parents are not using these safeguards and, most importantly, are not paying attention to how much TV their kids are watching.

One such safeguard is the V-chip, a feature on a television set that blocks out programs based on their ratings category. All thirteen-inch and larger televisions manufactured after January 2000 are required to have V-chip technology. For more information on the V-chip and television ratings system, log on to www.thetvboss.org.

According to recent studies, the amount of time our kids spend in front of the television is dangerous in itself. The Annenberg Public Policy Center suggested that children spend more time sitting in front of the TV than any other activity, with the exception of sleeping. Many experts have also connected television violence with real-life violence. Jeffrey Johnson of Columbia University observed that children who watched more than three hours a day of television were much more likely to engage in aggressive behavior as adults.[15] It may not just be the act of watching television that presents a problem. Bucknell University psychologist Chris Boyatzis suggested, "What may be going on is that families high in TV viewing are also lower in moral and character education."[16]

According to parentstv.org, the average child watches twenty-eight hours of television every week, an average of four hours per day. By the time a child finishes elementary school, he or she will have witnessed eight thousand murders on television. It's also reported that every four minutes, television and movie audiences witness an act of serious violence. That's frightening, to say the least. The level of violence during Saturday morning cartoons is higher than the level of violence during prime time. There are three to five violent acts per hour in prime time, versus twenty to twenty-five acts per hour on Saturday morning.[17] It's hard to believe, yet true!

In June 1999, the South Asian nation of Bhutan, located between India and China, lifted their ban on television and became one of the last countries in the world to receive this media mode. Those who could afford it subscribed to a cable service and paid five dollars per month, which provided forty-six channels of round-the-clock entertainment.

PBS's *Frontline* reported that children quickly began to neglect homework, and even Buddhist monks replaced their religious duties in favor of watching television. People's behavior began to drastically change for the worst. Gentle boys from good Buddhist families practiced body slams, imitating their new idols from the World Wrestling Federation. Three years after the arrival of television, Bhutan experienced what some called its first crime wave of murder, fraud, and drug offenses.

The *Guardian*, a Bhutan newspaper, stated, "We are beginning to see crime associated with drug users all over the world—shoplifting, burglary and violence."[18] A letter to the editor made perhaps the best summation: "Dear Editor, TV is very bad for our country . . . it controls our minds . . . and makes us crazy. The enemy is right here with us in our own living room. People behave like the actors and are now anxious, greedy, and discontent."[19] The national newspaper *Kuensel* recommended censoring television. Some critics have even asked that it be banned again.

In the same June 2003 issue of the *Guardian*, Sangay Ngedup, Bhutan's minister for health and education, said, "For the first time, children are confiding in their teachers of feeling manic, envious, and stressed. Boys have been caught mugging for cash. A girl was discovered prostituting herself for pocket money in a hotel in the southern town of Phuents-holing." It was also reported that one-third of Bhutan girls wanted to look more American. Almost the same percentage of girls drastically altered their views of traditional relationships—they preferred boyfriends over husbands and preferred sexual relations outside of matrimony. While the Bhutanese government did not officially blame television, they acknowledged its obvious influence.

Dr. Brandon Centerwall of the University of Washington conducted a study and noted the doubling of the homicide rate after the introduction of television in the United States. He concluded that "long-term childhood exposure to television is a causal factor behind approximately one-half of the homicides committed in the United States, or approximately 10,000 homicides annually."[20] Dr. Centerwall further estimated that as many as half of America's rapes and assaults could be related to television. Imagine—it might be possible to save up to 10,000 lives every year if we didn't have television.

What's most dangerous about violent television is that it strongly affects the particular segments of the population who are already vulnerable or who present at-risk behavior. Alfred Blumstein, dean of John Heinz School of Public Policy and Management at Carnegie-Mellon, noted that "the glorification of violence on television has little effect on most folks, but it has a powerful effect on kids who are poorly socialized . . . it dehumanizes them and becomes a self-fulfilling process."[21]

Highlander. On January 3, 1997, two seventeen-year-olds from Bellevue, Washington, Alex Baranyi and David Anderson, killed a family of four. Three of the family members were found dead in their home. All were beaten on the head with a blunt object and stabbed in the neck. The oldest daughter, Kimberly, twenty, was found savagely beaten and strangled to death in a nearby park.

When explaining the motivation for the crime, Alex told investigators that he planned to kill someone because he was in a rut. Both killers were deeply involved in the gothic lifestyle and had made a list of potential murder victims. Alex had a deep interest in fantasy role-playing games, collected weapons like swords and knives, and was a big fan of the science-fiction television series *Highlander*. He even wore his hair in a ponytail to emulate the star of the show, a sword-wielding superhero. Alex and David were each convicted of four counts of aggravated first degree murder and given a sentence of life with no chance of parole.

The Sopranos. In the late 1990s, HBO introduced a series about a mobster and his family called *The Sopranos*.

On January 14, 2003, after seeing a murder on this hit show, twenty-year-old Jason Bautista and his fifteen-year-old half brother, Matthew, choked, strangled, and beat their mother to death. They proceeded to chop off her head and hands and placed them in a duffel bag in their closet at home.

Jason and Matthew threw the rest of her body in a ravine. When Jason was arrested, he told investigators that he had seen an episode of *The Sopranos* where he saw the same type of dismemberment.

During his trial, Jason told the court that after years of being abused and subjected to unacceptable living conditions, he decided he had to do something about his mentally ill mother. He was convicted and received a sentence of twenty-five years to life. His accomplice received no sentence in exchange for his testimony against Jason.

Wrestling Mania. Gorman Roberts, a young man from Fort Lauderdale, Florida, pushed a five-year-old autistic child into a canal and let him drown on February 10, 2002. Gorman walked away laughing and told police later that the victim, a third child, and he had watched a *World Wrestling Entertainment* program that featured famous wrestler "the Rock" three days before the incident. Defense attorney Ellis Rubin said, "Little boys imitate what they see on TV. If they hadn't been watching wrestling, none of this might have happened." The attorneys were considering subpoenaing "the Rock" for the trial, claiming there was a connection between the incident and the violence portrayed in professional wrestling.

VIDEO GAMES: WHATEVER HAPPENED TO PACMAN AND DONKEY KONG?

Luke Woodham's infatuation with video games was certainly on a lesser scale than that of music, but in his words: "I did waste a lot of time on them that could have been better spent on other things." His favorite games were first-person shooter games like *Doom, Mortal Combat, Duke Nukem,* and *Quake.* He played *Doom* for hours at a time and received great satisfaction from going from one level to another by killing people and destroying anything in his path.

When I was growing up, video games were much more wholesome and fun. I remember getting my first home video game system, Atari, and finally being able to play my favorite games, *Tecmo Bowl* and *Galaga,* at home. Eventually I graduated to games that were more intricate in their graphic design, like *Pacman* and *Mario Brothers.*

I often tell teens that back then these games were so harmless you could play them with your parents and even your grandparents. One way to judge the amount of violent content in today's games is to have your child consider whether or not he or she would play the game with you. Most kids, unfortunately, would likely say no. It is quite a challenging feat today to find a game that doesn't include multiple acts of murder or bloodshed.

The video game market not only is a terrible source of entertainment for our children, but it is simply a cash cow. In 2003, video games generated $13.9 billion in revenue. That same year movie studios made $9.2 billion. That's quite a difference! *Halo 2*, by the way, sold more than $100 million on its first day of release.

Violent games enhance the problem of violent entertainment because you can manipulate the violence yourself. Lt. Col. David Grossman spoke to the New York state legislature about the connection between violent crime and violent video games:

> It is my professional opinion, and it is the opinion of major experts in this area, such as the American Medical Association, the American Psychiatric Association, the National Institute of Mental Health, the American Academy of Mental Health, and the Surgeon General, that based on extensive research, violent video games are harmful to children . . . The games that permit a child to hold and aim a gun and fire it at humans are particularly harmful, since these devices teach shooting skills. They are firearms training devices at best, and murder simulators at worst.

When something is both incredibly profitable and—according to numerous medical associations and professionals—dangerous to young children, I'm surprised our government has not created or enforced effective restrictions and protective laws for them. It seems that our country's lawmakers assume the video game community can police themselves. That's practically impossible, of course. How can these video game creators and distributors use good, moral judgment when all they see are dollar signs?

While I will do my best to describe a few of these games, it's much more impactful when you see with your own eyes the kind of violence that is being sold. I encourage you—as parents, teachers, and youth leaders—to play some of these games and make your own assessment. I'm sure your findings will cause you great concern.

GRAND THEFT AUTO

For years *Mario Brothers* dominated the video game sales charts and held the number one spot of best-selling video games. Around 2002, this game was dethroned and *Grand Theft Auto* took over the title. Although this series is technologically brilliant, its creators, Rock Star Games, have taken violence to an entirely new and disgusting level through its simulation of murder. *Grand Theft Auto* has sold more than 35 million copies and worldwide sales are rapidly approaching 2 billion dollars.

In this video game, you are required to complete missions ranging from spraying graffiti to murdering innocent people. As you carry out these assignments, you are involved in all kinds of illegal activity, such as obtaining various weapons (guns, chainsaws, and baseball bats), selling drugs, and having sex with prostitutes. Players are encouraged to kill the prostitutes after sex so they can get their money back.

The strategy guide for *Grand Theft Auto* reads, "You don't have to use the chainsaw to kill this guy, but it's oh so much fun, especially since he's so slow. Switch to your handgun or fists while running to catch up with him, then either plug him full of lead or flip fast to the chainsaw and cut him up good." There have been quite a few crimes associated with the *Grand Theft Auto* series. The case that has probably received the most media attention involved Devin Moore.

On June 7, 2003, Devin, eighteen, was being booked for stealing a car. While inside the Fayette, Alabama, police department, he wrestled a gun away from the booking officer and shot and killed him. Devin then shot another police officer at the station who was running to assist his fellow officer, and finally shot and killed a third person, a dispatcher. This *Grand Theft Auto* player continued doing what he did best and stole a police

Grand Theft Auto *player Devin Moore killed three police officers in Alabama.*

vehicle. When he was arrested four hours later, he remarked, "Life is like a video game . . . You've got to die sometime."[22]

Devin played the video game *Grand Theft Auto: Vice City* for hours every day. His attorneys used the damaging influence of video game violence in their defense strategy, but lost. Devin now resides on death row in Alabama. He told me he is writing a book about his life and said, "I'm directing my book at a younger audience and trying to explain how fast your whole life can be changed."

One night in 2002 in Wyoming, eighteen-year-old Michael Emery and his buddy Brian Davidson were playing *Grand Theft Auto* and drinking beer when they forged a plan to imitate the game in real life. They began their violent rampage by running over victim Jerry Steinberg with a car. Jerry was riding his bike when they slammed into him with their Honda and sent him flying to the ground. He was unconscious when his attackers returned a short time later, along with two females. The two men and one of the girls, sixteen-year-old Natasha Toothman, took turns stomping and punching the victim. Mr. Steinberg suffered at least twenty blows, and his injuries included a fractured skull, a broken nose, and four broken ribs.

Another potential victim was lucky to get out of the way when he was almost run over while walking home that night. He said the driver of the car, Brian, had "an angry look on his face."[23] Ironically, this potential victim owned a copy of *Grand Theft Auto* and commented that the near miss "felt like the same exact thing."[24] The attackers played *Grand Theft Auto* again the next day. They were arrested two days later.

MANHUNT

Even more troubling than the Grand Theft Auto series is a first-person shooter game called *Manhunt*. It allows you to take on the role of a serial killer named James Earl Cash. The plot of this game is that James escaped from death by lethal injection because a wealthy Hollywood director bribed the doctors to inject him with a sedative instead. You, as James, are commissioned to make snuff films and use the murders you commit as footage.

After you wait for the perfect time to attack, you are offered various ways to kill your victim, for example, strangulation by a plastic bag or cutting with a machete. When you kill people, you are shown multiple camera angles of the murder, and the Hollywood director audibly encourages you through your earpiece.

Manhunt has been banned from domestic sale in New Zealand. This has prompted other countries to question the sanity of selling this kind of game to troubled children. A reviewer of the video game commented, "It's one thing to talk about wires and machetes. It's another thing to see the animated scenes of a gang member . . . while his head is hacked off . . . Even the most hardened gamer will squint their eyes or grit their teeth as they watch these grisly deaths."[25]

On June 19, 2007, mtv.com posted a quote by David Cooke, director of the British Board of Film Classification, who said that *Manhunt 2* "is distinguishable from recent high-end video games by its unremitting bleakness and callousness of tone in an overall game context which constantly encourages visceral killing with exceptionally little alleviation."

Doom

Doom is another example of a video game that allows you to be the killer as you manipulate the main character in the game. You can look through the sights of a gun and experience the act of killing in a very realistic manner. This game is infamous for its extreme depiction of violence, gore, and satanic imagery, and has been called a "mass murder simulator" by Lt. Col. David Grossman. Columbine shooters Eric Harris and Dylan Klebold were avid players of the game, along with Pearl, Mississippi, shooter Luke Woodham.

Evan Ramsey, a teen from Bethel, Alaska, enjoyed regularly playing *Doom*. On February 19, 1997, he became one of the many teen killers in the 1990s school shooting rampage. Evan killed his principal and a student and wounded two others. His father, once imprisoned for violent assault and kidnapping charges, thought his son had purposely imitated the violent video game. Evan, at one point, had even told others that it would be cool to shoot up the school. The school shooting occurred a few weeks after his father was released from jail. Evan is currently serving a lengthy prison sentence with little chance at parole.

ARE WE TRAINING OUR KIDS TO KILL?

HALO

Doom and *Manhunt* are not the only controversial first-person shooter video games. Lee Boyd Malvo—one of the snipers responsible for the 2002 shootings in the Washington, D.C., area—trained on an Xbox video game called *Halo*. In this science fiction world, you become a superhuman soldier equipped with technologically savvy armor. You are able to switch the mode of play to sniper mode, which is how Lee played the game. In doing so, it is as though you are training to shoot.

One of the most well-known cases connecting video game violence to real-life murder is the school shooting in Paducah, Kentucky, in December 1997. Fourteen-year-old Michael Carneal opened fire on a prayer circle in the Heath High School cafeteria, killing three people and wounding five. Michael was said to be an avid player of first-person shooter video games and was also fascinated with guns. There were some reports that detailed the many arcade video games housed in his garage and the excessive amounts of time he spent playing them.

Michael was frequently bullied and probably reached his breaking point when the high school paper claimed he had feelings for another male student. Many of his classmates used this gossip as an opportunity to harass him even more. On December 1, a fed-up Michael broke down. He loaded a pistol in his backpack, hid two shotguns and a rifle under a blanket, and walked into the school. He began shooting at a group of students who were praying. Michael was unusually accurate with his targets and hit eight of eight shots. Three female students died that day, including his close friend Nicole Hadley. Five others were injured, including Missy Jenkins, who was paralyzed from the waist down.

Following the shooting, the FBI announced that Michael had shot like an expert marksman. He had a remarkably high level of accuracy and outperformed many trained police officers. So how does a kid with limited shooting experience become an expert marksman? Was it mere luck? Perhaps

Michael was "trained" to kill on murder simulators or, as we call them today, video games.

Forensic experts determined that this young man's shooting style at the school displayed specific techniques learned from video games—his accuracy, his stance, and how he fired only one round at each target, never taking his eyes off the person. Also, most of Michael's shots were aimed at the head or the upper body. In many video games, like *House of the Dead, Goldeneye, Grand Theft Auto, Doom,* and *Turok,* players are encouraged and even given bonus points for head shots.

Jack Thompson, a Miami attorney and an outspoken video-game violence expert, was interviewed on *World News Tonight with Peter Jennings* on October 11, 2002, and spoke about the United States Army's own sniper video game, similar to *Halo,* called *America's Army.* This recruiting tool is available on the army's Web site as a free download. It is used to train civilians as snipers. Thompson made a haunting statement when he told national audiences, "While the army was trying to catch Malvo and Muhammad, it was training new snipers to take their place."

Thompson gave further opinions: "The video game industry, even after Columbine, whose killers trained on *Doom,* has targeted American kids with violent games that train them to kill. These games are nothing more than adult-rated murder simulators that make killing foreseeable and likely."

Did you know that military training tools are practically identical to commercial video games? The U.S. Army has taken the basic Super Nintendo, replaced the plastic pistol with a plastic M-16, modified the targets that appear on the screen, and named it *Multipurpose Arcade Combat Simulator* or *MACS.* It is being used extensively for military marksmanship training. Similarly, the U.S. Marine Corps has licensed the first-person shooter game *Doom* and is using it to train their combat fire teams in tactics and to script and rehearse combat actions of killing.

Doesn't it seem odd that the video game industry can market these games to the military for combat purposes and then allege that they have no expectation the games could be potentially harmful to children? It's simple—video games are helping kids gain the skill and the will to commit murder!

HEAR WHAT THE EXPERTS HAVE TO SAY

A majority of medical and psychological professionals have agreed that exposing our children and young adults to violent entertainment is a hazard to their well-being. "Researchers found nonaggressive children who had been exposed to high levels of media violence had similar patterns of activity in an area of the brain linked to self-control and attention as aggressive children who had been diagnosed with disruptive behavior disorder."[26]

At a bipartisan congressional conference in 2000, the medical community, which included the American Medical Association and the American Academy of Pediatrics, submitted a joint statement:

> At this time, well over one thousand studies . . . point overwhelmingly to a causal connection between media violence and aggressive behavior in some children. The conclusion of the public health community, based on over thirty years of research, is that viewing entertainment violence can lead to increases in aggressive attitudes, values and behavior, particularly in children.

And in referring specifically to video games: "Preliminary studies indicate that the negative impact may be significantly more severe than that wrought by television, movies or music."[27]

A spokesperson from the American Psychological Association commented on the wealth of research supporting the causal relationship between media violence and real-life violence: "The evidence is overwhelming. To argue against it is like arguing against gravity."[28] According to a report published by the Federal Trade Commission: "The violence to which American children are exposed in the name of entertainment is having an effect on their values and behavior."[29]

Dr. Vincent P. Matthews, professor of radiology at Indiana University School of Medicine in Indianapolis, determined that "playing a certain type of violent video game may have different short-term effects on brain function than playing a nonviolent—but exciting—game."[30]

British researchers, in examining a variety of North American studies, have found that violent imagery does affect the thoughts and emotions of young people and increases the chance of them experiencing future aggressive or fearful behavior.[31]

SAFEGUARDS AND SOLUTIONS

The entertainment world seems convinced that warning labels and ratings help prevent underage individuals from accessing violent media. When it comes to pornography, for example, sexually explicit sites display a warning before a person is able to enter the Web site. Do you honestly think a pop-up warning screen will stop a hormone-driven teenager from browsing through a porn site? And are slapping ratings on video games without enforcing them enough to deter a teenager from buying a violence-laden game?

While warning labels and ratings systems are definitely good practices to have in place, retailers don't do a great job of enforcing them. In a survey reported by the Federal Trade Commission, for instance, only 55 percent of national stores asked a child's age when selling him an M (mature)-rated game.[32] Regional and local stores only asked for identification 35 percent of the time. It seems nobody cares about protecting our children! In movie theaters we all know that practically anyone can purchase a PG movie ticket and walk right into a different theater showing an R-rated film. Who is policing what minors watch after they buy a movie ticket?

We need to tighten up our obscenity laws and monitor what is sold to our children. If a brick-and-mortar or online music store is caught selling R- or X-rated music to children and young teenagers, its owners should be fined and prosecuted as if they were selling pornography to children. Quite frankly, much of this music is audio pornography. I also believe we need to set age limits for live music events. Minors are not allowed into porn shops or strip clubs, but are allowed to attend concerts, some of which may contain mature adult content.

When it comes to specifically rating video games, the system in place is embarrassingly inadequate. In a June 14, 2006, House subcommittee hearing titled "Violent and Explicit Video Games: Informing Parents and Protecting Children," elected officials criticized the Entertainment Software Ratings Board (ESRB) and video game retailers on the poor job they were doing with safeguarding kids from adult-themed video games.

The ESRB—a team in charge of ascertaining and applying appropriate ratings on every video game—base their ratings on information and video clips the game manufacturer gives them. At the hearing, an expert witness and associate professor at the Harvard School of Public Health said, "The ESRB's inability to play [each] game undermines their ability to independently rate the games, undermining the public's confidence in the ratings."[33]

The solution to the problem of marketing violent movies to minors is pretty simple, yet drastic. We need to eliminate the PG-13 movie rating. The PG-13 rating was created in an effort to keep R-rated violence away from children. Instead of protecting our children, however, this rating has become the very format to expose kids to perverted sex, obscenity, and violence. Most PG-13 movies have become watered-down versions of R-rated movies.

Writer Liza Mundy said, "One thing that's clear is that the PG-13 label has evolved into an advertisement: Studios use it to send a message to teenagers—and young kids who long to be teenagers—that the movie will contain cool stuff."[34] Tom Ortenberg, from Lionsgate Releasing, put in his two cents about the objectionable content: "I do believe that the MPAA allows too much violence and sexual content into PG and PG-13 movies. I believe they do it because they are bought and paid for by the studios whose movies they rate."[35]

All that being said, rating systems need to be enforced—period. We need to start making people accountable for what is being sold to our kids! You should know that I fully support free speech and the First Amendment. I believe that Americans have the right to produce violent, pornographic, and obscene entertainment. My main concern with our country's legal system is that we are failing to care for our children by allowing companies to market and sell this offensive material directly to them.

It's time we start writing to and pleading with our local, state, and national government leaders to do something about this problem. Make your voice known today and help me protect our children. Together we can help prevent more people from becoming victims at the hands of teen killers.

FOR MORE INFORMATION ON TEEN MURDER
AND THE CASES COVERED IN THIS BOOK,
LOG ON TO WWW.PHILCHALMERS.COM.
DON'T MISS PHIL'S BOOK,
THE ENCYCLOPEDIA OF TEEN KILLERS.

FIVE

BULLIED TO THE BREAKING POINT

> I feel like everyone is against me, but no one ever makes fun of
> me, mainly because they think I am a psycho. There is one kid
> above all others that I want to kill. I want nothing more than to
> put a hole in his head.
>
> —FROM THE WRITINGS OF KIP KINKEL,
> teen killer

Minutes before his school shooting, Luke Woodham handed a note to a friend. It contained his last message to the world in the event he was killed during the shooting.

> I am not insane, I am angry. I killed because people like me are mistreated every day. I did this to show society, push us and we will push back . . . All throughout my life, I was ridiculed, always beaten, always hated. Can you, society, truly blame me for what I do? Yes, you will . . . It was not a cry for attention, it was not a cry for help. It was a scream in sheer agony saying that if you can't pry your eyes open, if I can't do it through pacifism, if I can't show you through the displaying of intelligence, then I will do it with a bullet.[1]

When Luke and I met, he relived some of his childhood experiences and feelings of being picked on with a lot of emotional agony. "Every time I was bullied it was always a reminder that they [peers] didn't want me, that I'd never fit in, that I'd never be one of them. You go through life feeling like you're on the outside looking in. This rejection that I faced throughout life made me feel unable to ever open up to any individual."

Nobody wants to be rejected—and definitely not a young boy like Luke, who was devoid of self-confidence. Luke was an obvious target for bullies from elementary school all throughout high school. He was easy prey because he didn't even like himself. Luke was ashamed to be seen by people. He avoided public places as much as possible because he thought he looked like a freak. It was torture for him to have to walk through a crowded mall or even cut his own lawn because of his overwhelming fear of how others perceived him. He didn't want anyone to have to endure the image of an overweight, ugly, and repulsive boy who wore suspenders and thick eyeglasses.

The bullying began in his early years. Even before Luke reached junior high school, he dreaded going to school because every day kids made fun of his nerdy appearance. Not a day went by without Luke being teased or even physically assaulted. A schoolmate of his told the *Jackson Clarion-Ledger,* "I remember when he started kindergarten he was picked on every day. When we got to junior high he still got picked on. They called him fat, chunky, and chubby. And they used to jump him all the time."

Luke vividly remembered a time in the seventh grade when it was pouring rain. Instead of traveling underneath a walkway safe from the rain, he took the longer, water-drenched route to avoid being taunted by the popular kids. He did whatever it took to avoid being the center of the wrong kind of attention.

It got worse in high school. As Luke traveled the school hallways, the shouts from his peers would rattle his ears, "Last one to hit Luke is gay!" And hoards of guys would begin to pummel him with brutish force. Sometimes the mean-spirited kids would run up behind him, pull his pants down, and give him wedgies for all the kids to see. On many occasions, Luke had signs slapped on his back that read "Kick me" and "Hit me." And his fellow students obliged.

Luke tried to fight back several times, but because he was outnumbered, the other kids told the teacher that Luke had started it. Without fail, Luke always came out of these fights looking like the bad guy. He ultimately gave up and surrendered to the habitual kicking, pushing, hitting, and endless barrage of verbal assaults. The students treated him like garbage, the teachers looked away, and Luke dissolved into an emotional wasteland.

Luke told me that by the time of his involvement with the Kroth he "felt hollow and empty inside like . . . the walking dead." By the time his mental anguish became so bad that he was desperate for some form of intervention, it was too late. Luke said, "I had already pushed everyone so far away from me that there was no one to ask for help."

Luke has never solely blamed his crimes on being bullied, but he definitely figures it in as a significant contributing factor. He believes that there is only so much bullying a kid can take before he or she snaps. He also suggested that unless teachers, parents, and especially students open their eyes to the harmful consequences of bullying others, more school shootings will occur: "I'm not saying that it [school shootings] is the right thing to do, but obviously most of these kids don't see much of an alternative."

THE BULLYING PROFILE

So what is bullying, and how does it differ from typical joking behavior exhibited by juveniles? While bullying can mean a lot of different things, Professor Dan Olweus, the guru researcher of bullying among school-age children, defines it as when a young person "is exposed, repeatedly and over time, to negative actions on the part of one or more other students."[2]

Bullying can include doing or saying something to gain control of or have power over another person. This can be accomplished by calling other kids offensive names, saying or writing nasty things about them, threatening them, or even taking it to a physically menacing level by kicking or hitting them. Bullying can also mean making someone do something he doesn't want to do or even stealing something from him. It can be as indirectly malevolent as ignoring someone or purposefully leaving him out of an activity or a group of people.

In the 2005–2006 school year, about 28 percent of kids ages twelve to seventeen were bullied within six months.[3] *The Journal of the American Medical Association* recorded that one-third of American students experience bullying, either as a target or a perpetrator. Children victimized by bullies were reported by 47 percent of parents and 77 percent of teachers.[4]

Bullying and school violence have caused 160,000 fearful children to miss one or more school days each month.[5]

Research shows that the transition between elementary and middle school is the most brutal period of this activity, because at that time students undergo an increase in aggression. All of these alarming statistics and facts prove just how troubling this issue is, and expose the tremendous amount of fear that something as simple as going to school can bring.

Researchers have discovered that exposure to bullying is related to increased dropout rates, lower self-esteem, fewer friends, declining grades, and increases in illness. Miya Omori, EdD, wrote an article titled "Bullying: A New Sense of Need in the US Educational System" and concurred:

> Bullying not only affects children immediately, it also has long term debilitating effects on psychological well-being possibly leading to depression and low self-esteem in adulthood. The immediate effects include anxiety, depression, withdrawal and in some cases aggression. Victims of bullying tend to dislike school, causing them to avoid it or perform poorly.[6]

Bullies typically target weak victims and pick on them because of the frustration they are experiencing in their own lives. Experts conclude that boy bullies generally take it to a physical level, and girl bullies primarily use verbal slander or rejection. Most of these offenders suffer from depression and often have parents or guardians who apply inconsistent discipline in the home. Those who engage in bullying are likely to participate in future criminal activity, sexual harassment, and assault. Statistics show that male bullies are usually arrested for such crimes by the age of twenty-four.

CYBERBULLYING: BREAKING THE BORDERS OF SCHOOL WALLS

In light of the technology-driven environment we live in today, a new form of bullying has emerged. It doesn't take place at school, at the playground, or on the school bus. What is commonly referred to as "cyberbullying" happens in the comfort of a student's own home. With easy access to the Internet and available tools to create Web sites, post messages, and circulate pictures, young people are using this mode of communication to spread gossip about, verbally assault, and post embarrassing photos of their peers.

The Bergen County *Record* published several instances of this type of online mistreatment in 2004. In Garfield, New Jersey, for a period of two years, several classmates publicly humiliated on the World Wide Web a portly seventh grader with poor social skills. One student created a Web site mocking the seventh grader and also allowed other people to post hurtful messages about him. In Allendale, another New Jersey town, a Web site was built for students that named the school's "top five biggest homosexuals" and the "top twenty gayest guys and gayest girls."[7]

Amy Harmon of the *New York Times* wrote an article recognizing this prevalent activity.

> The technology, which allows its users to inflict pain without being forced to see its effect, also seems to incite a deeper level of meanness. Psychologists say the distance between bully and victim on the Internet is leading to an unprecedented—and often unintentional—degree of brutality, especially when combined with a typical adolescent's lack of impulse control and underdeveloped empathy skills.[8]

I-SAFE Inc., another nonprofit leader in Internet safety education, found that

- 42 percent of kids have been bullied while online; 1 in 4 has had it happen more than once.
- 35 percent of kids have been threatened online. Nearly 1 in 5 has had it happen more than once.
- 58 percent of kids admit someone has said mean or hurtful things to them online. More than 4 out of 10 say it has happened more than once.[9]

Parry Aftab, executive director of WiredSafety.org, a volunteer organization that provides global online safety, support, and education, said, "We're always talking about protecting kids on the Internet from adults and bad people. We forget that we sometimes need to protect kids from kids."[10]

THE BULLIED

Before their infamous killing rampage in Colorado, Eric Harris and Dylan Klebold were regularly picked on by fellow classmates. Many students, not necessarily those who had picked on them, paid dearly for these acts with their lives. In a home video shot by the teen killers, Dylan said, "I'm going to kill you all. You've been giving us sh— for years . . . You're f—ing going to pay for all the sh— . . . We don't give a sh— because we're going to die doing it." [11]

Luke Woodham revealed his deep-set anger against the effects of bullying when he said, "I am the epitome of all Evil! I have no mercy for humanity . . . They tortured me until I snapped and became what I am today."[12]

There are many school shooters and teen killers who have suffered from the traumatic effects of bullying to some degree. One of the earliest teen killers, Charles Starkweather, killed eleven people in Nebraska and Wyoming. Charles was born with bowed legs and suffered from a speech impediment that resulted in being teased and beaten up from an early age.

In another early school shooting that occurred in 1982 in Nevada, Patrick Lizotte opened fire in a psychology class. He killed the teacher and wounded two more students before fleeing the school. For twelve years, Patrick was constantly taunted and teased by his classmates and even his teachers. People made fun of him because of his Coke-bottle-thick eyeglasses, the jacket he wore to school every day, and the way he walked. Some students even threw basketballs at his head in gym class.

On the day of the murder, Patrick walked into the classroom, called out the teacher's name to get his attention, and pulled out a .22-caliber Sturm/Ruger revolver from his green army jacket. In the middle of the frightened teacher's vocal protest, Patrick fired one shot and killed him. Two other students were injured in the process. Patrick is currently serving a life sentence.

In 1993, fifteen-year-old Jason Michael Smith from Red Hill, Pennsylvania, got tired of nonstop bullying and shot his tormentor in the face. He used a 9mm automatic pistol and shot the bully in biology class. Reports showed that the victim had bullied Jason for two years before the shooting. Others had also picked on Jason since the second grade.

In 1994, ten-year-old James Osmanson from Butte, Montana, shot and killed a classmate on the playground of an elementary school. He used a .22 pistol. James was aiming for another boy but missed and shot eleven-year-old Jeremy Bullock behind the ear instead. James was teased because his parents were infected with the AIDS virus. James was sentenced in juvenile court and sent to the Pine Hills School for Boys. He has since been released.

Evan Ramsey, who murdered two people in Alaska in 1997, told a reporter from CBS's *60 Minutes*, "My main objective of going into the high school was to check out, to commit suicide." This bullied student suffered from severe depression and felt that no one understood the rejection he felt. On a daily basis, classmates called him names like "retard," "spaz," and "brain-dead." One of his victims was a school football player who daily teased him.

Kip Kinkel was a victim of bullying and was harassed mainly for his small size. His writings descriptively reveal the mind of a bullied teenager. "I feel like everyone is against me . . . mainly because they think I am a psycho. There is one kid above all others that I want to kill. I want nothing more than to put a hole in his head. The one reason I don't: Hope. That tomorrow will be better. As soon as my hope is gone, people die." He later added, "I sound so pitiful. People would laugh at this if they read it. I hate being laughed at. But they won't laugh after they're scraping parts of their parents, sisters, brothers, and friends from the wall of my hate."

In 2003, John Jason McLaughlin shot two students as he left the locker room of his Minnesota high school. When police asked what his plans were that day, he responded, "I was going to shoot some people" because "they were teasing me all the time."[13]

(left) *The arrest photo of Cold Spring, Minnesota, school shooter John Jason McLaughlin, who shot and killed two students at school, one by accident.*

(center) *John Jason McLaughlin, as he looks today in prison.*

(right) *The weapon used by school shooter John Jason McLaughlin. The reason for the shooting, according to Jason, was that he was being bullied by his murder victim. Others have said that Jason wasn't bullied or teased by any classmates.*

WHAT CAN WE DO?

Shocking? In an era and a country where our kids are raised in such a violent and obscene youth culture, it shouldn't surprise us that they are using violence and murder to solve their problems. To those who are being harassed at school, killing innocent people isn't a scary crime with weighty consequences. It has become a method for relief from bullying or a means to gain recognition other than being considered a "loser."

Numerous national law enforcement studies expose the leading cause of school shootings as bullying. In my research, I have also determined that bullying is present in many teen killers' lives, especially most of the ones I have personally interviewed and communicated with. It seems to me that teens today are not only sick and tired of getting bullied and tormented at school, but they are very angry that the respective officials in their schools and local communities are not protecting them.

One of my objectives in writing this book is to bring the problem of bullying to the forefront. This is a serious problem that demands immediate attention to prevent future school shootings. Luke Woodham shares my opinion. He told me:

> In all of the school shootings that I've studied, bullying was a factor. The kids felt like they were at the end of their rope and did something very drastic about it. Until steps are taken, not just by teachers and parents, but by kids themselves to reduce bullying, these shootings will continue. We all need to be responsible for ourselves and others. We all need to hold ourselves accountable for what we do. We are all in this together and we need to act like it. I understand that if all of us school shooters would have felt that way we wouldn't have killed anybody. But if the people who bullied us had felt the same way, we never would have been pushed to the point to act.

What can be done about this problem? Did you know that countries like England, Norway, and Sweden have implemented proven, antibullying programs in their educational institutions? Some international governments legally require schools to have an antibullying plan.

England, for instance, is a great role model for their proactive involvement in this crisis. One of the measures they have in place is handing out cards to each student listing information and phone numbers for various support groups. These resources provide access to adults whom bullied kids can talk to and get help. Because many kids feel especially embarrassed about admitting this problem to parents or teachers, we should similarly create a safe environment or provide them with an alternate arena where they can openly discuss their feelings before it becomes too late. As parents and teachers, we need to constantly remind children and teenagers to tell an adult of any problems they may be facing. It is our responsibility to do whatever it takes so students understand that bullying is not behavior that will be ignored or taken lightly.

I am advocating that schools begin to hand out more serious punishment for the students who bully others. I firmly believe that bullying is just as deadly as bringing a weapon to school, and the punishment should, therefore, be just as severe. We should give lengthy suspensions to bullies and expulsion from school for repeat offenders. If these hostile youths do not recognize the severity of their actions, nothing will prevent them from continuing their harmful conduct.

I also have determined that a lack of adult supervision in school environments allows this type of misconduct to flourish. The schools that seem to have a handle on bullying have a very strong presence of adults in the hallways, cafeterias, and on the outside of the school. These teachers and hall monitors police the common areas and take appropriate action when they see this type of behavior taking place. Another major plus is to have law enforcement personnel and school resource officers patrolling school hallways to deter student abuse. This would not only deter bullying but could also prevent other forms of school violence.

We must all rally to get government officials and schools to effectively diminish violent bullying. It has a tremendously negative effect on those who are mistreated and can result in irreparable and deadly consequences.

Jeremy Getman's journal echoed the emotional damage he endured when he addressed his tormentors and wrote, "Thanks to your arrogance, stupidity, and relentless torment that you have caused me for pushing me away and teasing me in elementary school . . . for making sure that every minute of school was hell for me—"[14]

Do something to stop bullying, and I'm sure you will not only help ensure a healthy school environment, but it's very possible you may divert another school massacre.

FOR MORE INFORMATION ON TEEN MURDER
AND THE CASES COVERED IN THIS BOOK,
LOG ON TO WWW.PHILCHALMERS.COM.
DON'T MISS PHIL'S BOOK,
THE ENCYCLOPEDIA OF TEEN KILLERS.

SIX

GUNS—THE ALL-AMERICAN PASTIME: A LOOK AT GUNS AND GUN CONTROL

> But we do know what happens when there is no one with a
> concealed weapon in these situations: people die.
>
> —CLARK APOSHIAN,
> Chairman of the Utah Shooting Sports Council,
> on the outcome of a public shooting spree

When you want to spark controversy concerning teen violence, all you have to do is mention the word *gun*. Guns have a way of dividing a crowd, and because it is such a hot and controversial topic, many politicians have it at the forefront of their agendas.

Guns, or firearms, were invented somewhere around the 1200s. Up until the 1960s, anyone could purchase a gun without being questioned, even teenagers. Back in the olden times, you could walk into a bank with your shotgun, lean it against the counter to conduct your financial business, and when you were finished, grab your gun and walk out! Students in the 1960s used to bring their guns into school for show-and-tell. Things have sure changed since then.

In this chapter, we will talk about these changes and explore the real issues surrounding these weapons. I want to assure you that I have no ulterior motive when it comes to this subject. I am only bringing to the table my many years of personal experience with guns, the extraordinary amount of time I have spent with law enforcement officials, and thousands of hours of research and study.

GUNS: GOOD OR BAD?

The first question we must ask is, are guns bad? The answer is a combination of yes and no. Because guns were created to do one thing—kill—they are bad when they end up in the hands of small children, the mentally ill, intoxicated individuals, untrained handlers, and bad people (like murderers and violent criminals). Guns give these people the opportunity to kill more people faster than if they used a knife or a baseball bat as a weapon.

Earlier I talked about the Springfield, Oregon, school shooter Kip Kinkel. Kip's parents were pulling their hair out trying to keep him occupied with positive activities to keep him out of trouble. But Kip developed a fascination with guns, explosives, firecrackers, and bombs, which he built and hid in a crawl space at home. One time, during a class project, he read aloud from a journal about his plans to kill everybody. He was obviously one troubled teen.

A recent photo of Springfield, Oregon, mass murderer Kip Kinkel, who is being led into the courthouse in Salem, Oregon, on June 20, 2007. Kinkel is trying to get a new trial.

So what did his parents do? Prompted by a suggestion from a counselor, they bought Kip a semiautomatic rifle and a semiautomatic handgun. They believed doing so would help them bond with their son. And what did Kip do? He killed his parents and two students at school and injured twenty-five others with the same "bonding" weapons his parents had purchased for him. Clearly, there was no legitimate reason for Kip to have access to these weapons. He was already a disturbed boy, and his mental anguish and inner rage were only charged by his fascination with and use of weapons. A gun was the last thing that belonged in Kip's hands.

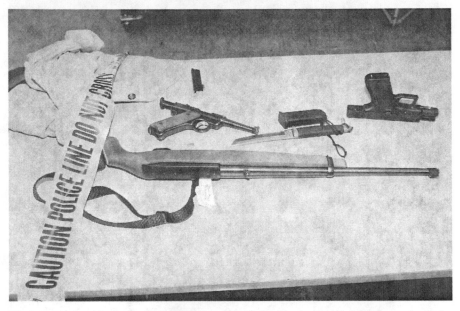

The weapons used in the Springfield, Oregon, school shooting by Kip Kinkel. He was obsessed with guns and knives, and even law enforcement authorities are surprised at some of the weapons and acessories that Kinkel was able to purchase and hide from his parents.

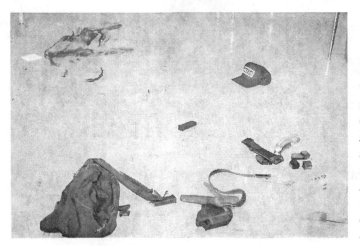

The aftermath of the Springfield, Oregon, school shooting. Note the belongings of the mass murderer Kip Kinkel, including the banana gun clip and the Nine Inch Nails hat.

When are guns good? I am convinced guns can be positive things when handled by two particular groups of people: law enforcement officers and trained civilians. In speaking of law enforcement, I am referring to police officers, detectives, secret service representatives, security personnel, and those hired to protect people and fight crime. Trained civilians are public persons who are trained and licensed to carry a concealed weapon at a legal age.

When our safety and our lives are being threatened, whom do we call for help? Do we call the dogcatcher so he can show up with his net to trap the bad guy? Do we call the fire department so they can rush to the scene with their fire hoses and spray the bad guy with water? Of course not. We call the police department, and we call them for one reason only. In this country they carry guns, and those guns can be used to threaten, disarm, or shoot to kill the bad guy who has targeted us for rape, assault, or murder.

Although I am a devoted and loyal supporter of law enforcement, I must point out a few facts. First, most police officers carry guns to protect themselves, not you. Second, police officers act as historians for the most part. This means that a majority of the time they show up after a crime has been committed with the responsibility to reconstruct the crime and, hopefully, apprehend or find the guilty party. This, of course, does little for you if you have been killed, raped, or wounded in a violent crime.

GUN CONTROL

So what's the deal with gun control? Many assume that if we get guns off the streets, we will be safer, or if fewer guns are made available, there will be proportionately fewer incidences of crime. Common sense should tell you these are foolish theories. If we banned guns tomorrow, for instance, and ordered all Americans to turn in their weapons by the end of the month and exacted punishment for those who refused, who do you think would turn in their weapons? The good guys, of course! The bad guys will never give up their firearms under any circumstances.

Do you remember how successful it was when alcohol was banned in the United States? Not very successful. Believe me, anyone who wanted a drink at that time could find one somewhere. It became a profitable business for underground criminals. The same thing would happen with banning firearms. All we would be doing is putting more money in the wallets of the bad guys. And furthermore, if banning weapons is the answer, why don't we just ban crime and be done with it?

A handful of countries have tried to ban weapons, including Jamaica, Australia, Great Britain, France, Germany, Switzerland, and Canada. In the nations where strict gun control laws were put in place, the opposite of the intended result occurred—the murder and violent crime rates increased! In 2002, for example, *USA Today* reported that after they banned guns in Australia, armed robberies rose by 51 percent, unarmed robberies by 37 percent, assaults by 24 percent, and kidnappings by 43 percent. While murders fell by 3 percent, manslaughter rose by 16 percent. According to a *BBC News* article self-explanatorily titled "Handgun Crime 'up' Despite Ban," handgun crime rose by 40 percent in the two years after it passed its gun ban in 1997.

Professor John Lott, a resident scholar at the American Enterprise Institute, wrote the book *More Guns, Less Crime,* which details this phenomenon. He proposed that countries that offer concealed-carry laws versus firearms-ban laws are statistically safer. He also proved that most criminals are afraid of being shot by armed civilians.[1]

Unlike these other countries, America has been slowly moving in the direction of allowing civilians to carry a concealed, deadly weapon. According to the National Rifle Association, more than 3 million Americans currently have a permit to carry a firearm. And consider this: both the violent crime and homicide rates are on the decline.

There are three main purposes for a gun—competitive target shooting, hunting animals, and self-preservation. I know some people feel queasy about the idea of hunting and shooting animals, especially when they picture Bambi at the mercy of a gruff, burly hunter with a shotgun. I hope that people who hunt will do so in as humane a manner as possible and without the intention of killing animals just for sport.

As far as self-preservation is concerned, I believe that the best possible protection and the ultimate insurance for defending your life is a gun. You can learn karate or carry around pepper spray or mace, but the only thing that can create a level playing field against a criminal with a gun is a gun. Simply put, it's a human equalizer.

Many people have died because they didn't believe in owning guns and had no way to stop the criminal that terrorized, raped, tortured, or killed them. And many people have lost loved ones because they had no weapon with which to defend them. That may sound somewhat cruel or presumptuous, but if you investigated some violent crime scenes or spoke to a few violent offenders, you would probably find yourself agreeing with me.

I respect all opinions on this matter, but I don't believe conservative gun control laws or a ban on them would be effective. Do I believe in some sort of gun control? Of course I do. I truly feel, for instance, that we should restrict the use and sale of guns to certain groups of people. I'm also definitely a big fan of mandating thorough background checks and imposing a waiting period before a person can procure a gun. We need to find effective ways to make it difficult for the bad guys and the wrong people to get hold of these weapons, whether in stores or on the streets.

Although it's a scary thought, we must keep in mind that every bad guy who wants a gun will get one somehow, somewhere. Every teen killer and serial killer I have spoken to has told me that nothing could have prevented them from getting a weapon, no matter what kinds of laws were imposed. These are just the facts. I'm sure that many politicians and government officials address the importance of gun control to make voters feel better or safer, even though the laws may not be working so well. It's time to stop making us feel good and start looking at the facts. It's time to tackle this problem and begin doing something to protect us.

GUN SECURITY

Gun security is the number one issue we need to be concerned with when dealing with guns and teen killers. Gun owners must be constantly reminded how to secure their weapons at home, thereby keeping them out of the hands of children or would-be teen killers. It's time to start holding gun owners accountable if they do not properly guard their weapons. If people want the right to own a deadly weapon, they must also be held legally responsible for proper storage of their firearms. In my home, all my weapons are stored in a metal box with a combination finger lock. It is virtually impossible for anyone besides me to have access to my weapons.

(top, left) *This is the type of gun safe Phil recommends for those who own rifles and shotguns and is much safer than the old gun cabinets made of cheap wood and glass.*

(top, right) *This is an example of a gun safe that can be purchased at any sporting goods store. It allows you to keep your handguns safe, but also have quick access to them with a push-button combination.*

(left) *This is what a gun cabinet looks like in a typical American home. Manufactured wood and a thin sheet of glass do nothing to protect deadly weapons.*

It is horrifying to see, however, the ways that many gun owners store their weapons. They usually place their guns and ammunition in a closet, a dresser drawer, or in an unsecured gun cabinet that is typically constructed of cheap wood and a glass front. Boy, nothing stops a criminal from accessing a weapon better than a thin piece of breakable glass! When you store weapons in this manner, you are basically inviting someone to not only take them but also possibly use them against you. It's too easy not to! Practically all school shooters, for example, acquired their weapons either at their own homes or at a friend's or neighbor's home. Let's look at a few of these young people and learn about the methods they used to acquire weapons.

SCHOOL SHOOTERS AND GUNS

On October 9, 2006, at Memorial Middle School in Joplin, Missouri, a thirteen-year-old seventh grader carried an assault rifle to school in a lawn chair bag. After pulling the gun out, he aimed it at the staff and fellow students, and fired one round into the ceiling. Before shooting anyone, his gun jammed. He quickly bolted out of the school and was apprehended. This boy was fascinated with the Columbine massacre and at the time of the attack was wearing a trench coat and a mask over his face. He allegedly begged his victims not to make him go through with the shooting.

His weapon of choice was a Mac 90 assault rifle, which is a replica of an AK-47, a semiautomatic high-velocity rifle. How do you think a teenage boy in middle school got his hands on a gun like this? From his parents, of course. While his parents did a good job of locking the weapon in a safe, their teenage son knew the combination. This is a good lesson to all of us who own guns and store them in a combination lock box. It may seem obvious, but only you should know the combination.

Luke Woodham took a Marlin .30-30 lever-action rifle to school that he obtained from his home. The gun was owned by his older brother and kept in an unlocked closet. The Columbine shooters, Eric Harris and Dylan Klebold, used several weapons. They illegally purchased some of them, and others were borrowed from a friend. Kip Kinkel used his own weapons from home, including a .22 Ruger rifle, a 9mm Glock pistol, and a .22 Ruger pistol.

Fayetteville, Tennessee, school shooter Jacob Davis shot and killed another student in the parking lot using his father's .22 Marlin bolt-action rifle. The police said the gun was regularly stored leaning against a bedroom wall. Edinboro, Pennsylvania, shooter Andrew Wurst, who shot up a middle

(AP Photo / Jefferson County Sheriff's Department)

(**left**) *Columbine mass murderers Eric Harris and Dylan Klebold caught on school security tape in the high school cafeteria during their shooting spree. Note Klebold's weapon of choice, the TEC-9.*

(**right**) *Prison photo of Tennessee school shooter Jacob Davis, who shot and killed another student in a dispute over a girl at his Fayetteville, Tennessee, high school.*

school dance, opened fire with a .25 Raven pistol taken from his father's dresser drawer.

In Jonesboro, Arkansas, thirteen-year-old Mitchell Johnson and eleven-year-old Andrew Golden opened fire on their classmates with guns—a .30-06 Remington rifle, a Universal .30 carbine, and a Ruger .44 magnum rifle—stolen from Andrew's grandfather, a licensed gun dealer. Police reported there was no forced entry into the man's gun storage room. Isn't it disturbing to realize how easily these school shooters acquired their weapons? Mitchell and Andrew were released on their twenty-first birthdays. Mitchell was arrested again shortly afterward for possessing a loaded handgun and drug possession and is awaiting sentencing at the writing of this book.

SCHOOL SAFETY

Have you ever asked yourself the question, why do teens bring guns to school to commit their acts of violence? Why not other places, like malls, football games, or field trips? Also, why don't teens shoot up police departments or army bases? I believe that teens carry out mass murders at schools because they know the likelihood of anyone having a gun to stop them from carrying out their crime is slim to none. Places like malls and even football games are littered with armed security or police officers. The same applies, of course, to police stations or army bases.

Very few schools that have experienced a mass shooting had armed police officers stationed at the school. The school in Red Lake, Minnesota, that school shooter Jeff Weise stormed had two security personnel, but neither was armed. (One of them was murdered.) The only way Luke Woodham was stopped was when a teacher ran to his own car, retrieved his handgun, and subdued Luke before he could hurt any more people, including himself.

Until we have armed security or police officers at every school, we will continue to put our children at risk. We need to legally and financially invest in school security. In Israel, they take the safety of their children very seriously. Their schools are protected like fortresses. Armed guards are posted on school buses, at field trips, and even at sporting events. America could learn a thing or two from Israel.

This is much too complicated an issue for us to cover in a few paragraphs, but there are some safeguards we should consider in promoting the safety of our schools: Lock all exterior doors down with alarms and video cameras. Place cameras on the front doors. Place armed police officers at the front of the school, who also patrol the exterior of the building.

My good friend Lt. Col. David Grossman has many great things to say on his Web site—www.killology.com—about keeping schools safe. Our hope is that we make our schools safer before more school shootings occur. If not, rest assured, the massacres will continue.

LEGAL CONCEALED WEAPONS

I am a big believer in the freedom to carry concealed weapons with the proper checks and the correct training. As I've said before, a trained civilian with a deadly weapon is the best hindrance to crime that I know. Former president of the American Sociological Association Peter Rossi conducted an in-depth study into the research of gun control. Among other fascinating findings, he and his colleagues concluded that civilian gun ownership is a deterrent against some crime. In his interviews with hundreds of convicted felons in state correctional systems, he also found that three-fifths of the prisoners said they would not attack a potential victim whom they knew to be armed. Two-fifths of them had even decided not to carry out a particular crime because they had a feeling the potential victim might have been armed.[2]

When someone breaks into your home, the chances of the police showing up to stop the attack before you are hurt or killed are pretty low. Many times there is not enough time to dial 911, and police will arrive just in time to take postmortem photos of the body, gather forensic evidence, and begin looking for the bad guy who committed the terrible crime.

The bad guys would rather nobody carry weapons except police officers, because then they would become pretty successful at carrying out their violent crimes. Things get a little more confusing for criminals when civilians are secretly carrying guns, because they can only guess who has one. Following are a few examples of armed civilians who could have been beaten, raped, or murdered but are alive today to tell their stories—thanks to the fact that they were legally carrying and concealing a firearm.

In a 2007 shooting in a Utah mall, eighteen-year-old Sulejmen Talovic marched into the crowded shopping center with a shotgun and a .38-caliber pistol hidden in his trench coat, a handful of ammunition in his backpack, and a will to kill. He showered a particular area of the mall with bullets killing five people and wounding four others. Many more would have been killed had it not been for an off-duty police officer who happened to be nearby eating dinner with his wife.

When this officer heard the gunshots, he pulled out his concealed weapon, confronted the gunman, and exchanged gunfire with him until other officers arrived. Sulejmen was ultimately killed in the shootout. In the wake of this tragedy, Clark Aposhian, chairman of the Utah Shooting Sports Council, made the following statement after admitting that it was impossible to determine if every violent confrontation could be avoided or stopped by a concealed-weapon holder: "But we do know what happens when there is no one with a concealed weapon in these situations: people die."[3]

In another Utah incident, a man broke into a home at about one in the morning and attacked the homeowner. Awakened by the commotion, the victim's grown son retrieved a small-caliber pistol and shot the intruder, wounding him in the abdomen, chest, and arm. The injured attacker fled the home and ran to a nearby residence, where he fell in the backyard in critical condition.

An intruder attacked a seventy-nine-year-old homeowner in his home in Franklinton, Ohio. The intruder violently knocked the elderly gentlemen to the floor, but the victim pulled out his gun in time and shot the criminal in the chest. The attacker ran out of the house, collapsed in an alley, and later that night was pronounced dead at a hospital.

A group of three armed intruders broke into the home of a Houston family, grabbed the family's twelve-month-old daughter, and threw the hysterical baby down a flight of stairs. One of the intruders then pulled out a gun. The father of the family successfully wrestled it away from him and shot and injured the trespasser. A second intruder quickly reacted and pulled out his own gun, and the father repeated the action. This time the dad killed the perpetrator. The remaining two assailants, one injured, fled the home and were soon arrested. The baby did not sustain life threatening injuries.

Perhaps the best example of an armed citizen protecting himself from becoming a murder victim involved teen killers Robert Tulloch and James Parker, whom I wrote about in the first chapter. Robert and James were desperate for money to move to Australia. They figured the best way to achieve their dream would be to rob and kill someone. On a murder mission, the duo even prepared for the crime by digging a grave near an abandoned home. They targeted a victim who lived only a few blocks away from this grave, in a wealthy suburban neighborhood, and schemed to rob the homeowner, kill him, and bury him in the grave. This was the first attempt at their plan.

Dressed in black and armed with army knives, duct tape, and zip ties,

Prison photo of Robert Tulloch, who, along with codefendant James Parker, stabbed to death two Dartmouth professors. There would have been an earlier victim, but he was a gun owner and showed them his weapon. Because of that decision, that gun owner is alive today.

Prison photo of New Hampshire teen killer James Parker, who, with codefendant Robert Tulloch, stabbed to death two Dartmouth professors in their own home.

Robert and James drove to the home of the potential victim, dug a grave behind the home to bury him, and cut his phone lines. James then hid in the bushes at the side of the home, and Robert calmly went to the front door and rang the doorbell. His game plan was to tell the victim his car had broken down and ask if he could use the telephone. Once inside, he would pull out his knife and subdue the homeowner. Then James would enter the home, rob the victim of his credit cards, and finally kill him. Should anyone else be home at the time, they were to die as well. Robert made sure they both knew that there were to be no witnesses.

Unfortunately for the budding psychopaths, this murder didn't go as planned. When the homeowner answered the door, he was somehow already feeling suspicious and held a handgun in plain view for Robert to see. Startled, Robert muttered some words and immediately left. Following his lead, James walked out of the bushes, and the two fled the neighborhood. The teen killers began to look for a victim who was against guns and didn't own one. They found their victims eight days later in the city of Dartmouth, Vermont.

The two killers posed as college students who were conducting a survey. A couple who were college professors invited the young men into their home. Robert and James viciously stabbed the couple to death and stole their credit cards and almost four hundred dollars in cash. These two guys were not quite that brilliant though, and left a knife sheath at the victims' home as they fled. Police were able to track them down from this piece of evidence, and they were eventually arrested and convicted of their heinous crime. This crime spree was referenced as "the Dartmouth Murder" and not "the Vershire Murder" because the Vershire homeowner had a gun, which saved his life. Robert and James were convicted of first degree murder and sentenced to life in prison without the eligibility of parole.

BASEBALL BAT CONTROL?

Many teen killers use other weapons besides guns. They have used baseball bats, crowbars, kitchen knives, trophies, fire, pocketknives, rope, wire, and whatever else they could get their hands on. Some don't use weapons—only their bare hands. Do we start a new campaign for baseball bat control? How about steak knife control? You see, as silly as it sounds, it is not the weapon we need to control, but the user. I cannot emphasize this enough.

Every home in America has a deadly weapon in it. That's right, *every home!* Many teen killers who show up at someone's home to rob or kill him use whatever weapon they can find in the kitchen drawers, like a butcher knife. The real concern here is not whether to control or ban guns, but to find out why teens are killing and start addressing and resolving those issues.

THINK ABOUT IT

Though I'm not a fan of mass e-mails, a friend forwarded one to me some time ago that I really enjoyed. It said that there are 80 million gun owners in America and 1,500 accidental gun deaths per year. The e-mail continued with the following information. There are also 700,000 doctors in the United States who cause 120,000 accidental deaths per year. So, statistically speaking, doctors are 9,000 times more dangerous than gun owners. The e-mail concluded, "Remember, guns don't kill people; doctors do. Please alert your friends to this alarming threat. We must ban doctors before this gets completely out of hand."

I hope you can see the humor and, of course, the truth in that illustration. It's easy to place blame on anyone or anything that conveniently suits your agenda, but let's get to the heart of the real problems and do our part to stop senseless murders and save innocent lives.

FOR MORE INFORMATION ON TEEN MURDER
AND THE CASES COVERED IN THIS BOOK,
LOG ON TO WWW.PHILCHALMERS.COM.
DON'T MISS PHIL'S BOOK,
THE ENCYCLOPEDIA OF TEEN KILLERS.

SEVEN

"WE, THE JURY, FIND THE DEFENDANT—": THE PUNISHMENT OF TEEN KILLERS

> While a fourteen or seventeen year old knows the difference
> between right and wrong, they don't have the same abilities to
> control their behaviors and assess risks the way adults do.
>
> —STEVEN DRIZIN,
> Northwestern University law professor,
> commenting on juvenile brain development

Rejecting an insanity defense, on June 12, 1998, a jury found Luke Woodham guilty of two counts of murder and seven counts of aggravated assault. Jurors deliberated for about five hours before reading their verdict. At the sentencing hearing, Luke spoke these words: "I am sorry for the people I killed and hurt. The reason you see no tears anymore is because I've been forgiven by God. If they could have given the death penalty in this case, I deserve it."[1]

Judge Samac Richardson gave Luke two consecutive life sentences for the murder convictions and seven twenty-year sentences for the aggravated assault convictions. Luke will never leave the Mississippi State Prison alive.

Here is what Luke had to say about his sentence:

It is hard to say what I deserve. Anyone in prison wishes that they had a lesser sentence, but I guess that I have to ask myself if I really deserve it. I am guilty

(AP Photo / Rogelio Solis)

Pearl, Mississippi, school shooter Luke Woodham being escorted into court wearing a bulletproof vest to face charges of killing his mother and two female students and wounding seven others.

of the crimes that I am in here for. I was out of my head when I did them, but I still did them. Would a mental institution have been fair? Considering my age and the mental state that I was in at the time that I committed my crime, I have to say that it could have been. I was the first person that I know of to be sent to prison for a school shooting and I still don't think anyone else has been given as much time as I have. (I have seen people get a life sentence but none of them got three life sentences plus one hundred and forty years.) . . . I would say that a lesser sentence could have been fair.

I think that the best thing for kids who commit violent crimes is a mental institute. This society has gotten to the point where all that they see is a bunch of "juvenile monsters." But what society needs to ask itself is *How did these young children become monsters?* A lot of the children who commit school shootings are abused, not necessarily at home but out in society. They have no way to respond healthily to the abuse by their peers

(*above*) The aftermath of the Cold
Spring, Minnesota, school shooting
committed by John Jason McLaughlin
that left two students dead.

(*right*) High School wrestling photo of
Louis Hamlin, who killed a 12-year-old
girl when he was only fifteen-years-old.

Missouri death row inmate Christopher Simmons, who bound and duct taped an elderly female and threw her over a bridge in Missouri. The elderly victim drowned in the river below.

The bridge from which Christopher Simmons threw his victim.

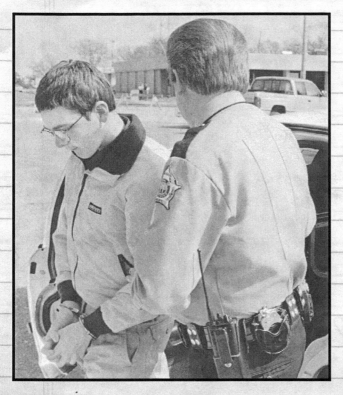

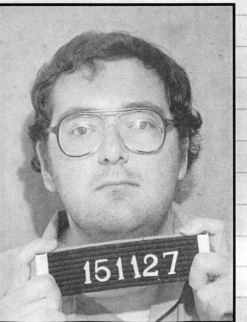

(above) Photo of Paducah, Kentucky, school shooter Michael Carneal heading into court. Carneal shot into a prayer circle at his high school, killing three and wounding five. Carneal was an avid fan of violent video games.

(right) Prison photo of Paducah, Kentucky, school shooter Michael Carneal as he looks today.

Ryan Atteberry, the first shooting victim of Springfield, Oregon, school shooter Kip Kinkel. Ryan was shot once in the face, but survived.

The class photo of Keith Johnson, taken moments before he killed another student in his school with a handgun. The other students had been bullying and threatening Johnson for weeks both at school and away from school.

(above) Kip Kinkel is led into Marion County Courthouse in Salem, Oregon, on June 20, 2007.

(right) Springfield, Oregon, school shooter Kip Kinkel's home, where he separately murdered his parents as they arrived home from work.

Edward O'Brien Jr., stands handcuffed in Somerville District Court on August 28, 1995, during a bail hearing.

(AP Photo / Patrick Whittemore, Pool)

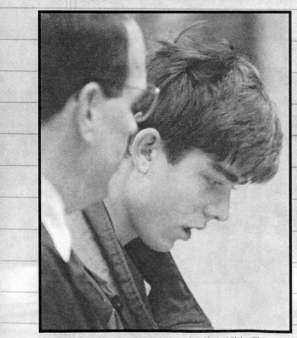

Moses Lake, Washington, school shooter Barry Loukaitis at a bail hearing. He was convicted of shooting four students and killing three at the age of 14. Barry was constantly bullied at school, and one of his murder victims was a teacher.

(AP Photo / Elaine Thompson)

Serial killer Jeffrey Dahmer makes his first courtroom appearance in Milwaukee, Wisconsin. Dahmer began his killing spree in Bath, Ohio, as a teenager. When Dahmer was arrested, they found body parts of eleven men in his apartment.

Columbine mass murderers Dylan Klebold and Eric Harris filming a school project in which they gun down fellow students at school. It's surprising that a violent project like this caused no concern with the police or school leaders, although this is one of the top predictors for future violence.

(left) An example of a death row prison yard, this one located at San Quentin in California. This is the type of exercise cage that murderer Todd Rizzo gets to exercise in a few times per week.

(below) A group of inmates at Mississippi State Penitentiary are honored for graduating from Bible Seminary. Included in the class is teen killer Ben Darras, seated in the front row, second from left. Darras and his girlfriend Sarah Edmondson went on a multi-state crime spree that left one dead and another paralyzed.

(AP Photo / Eric Risberg, POOL)

and it just builds up inside of them, anger and depression become a way of life for them, finally they get enough and release what was inside of them, then they get abused again, this time by the criminal justice system . . . So I think the best answer for cases like mine is to send the child to a mental institute, not to throw him away in a prison for the rest of his life where he will get no help.

When a teen commits a violent crime like murder, what are we, as a society and a government, supposed to do? How do we determine appropriate recompense for their wrongs? Does sticking them behind bars really make a difference in rehabilitating them? And what is the appropriate age for a child to be tried and convicted as an adult? This is a particularly controversial issue.

The first question we must ask is a simple one: do teenagers think about the repercussions of their crimes before they kill? The answer is a resounding *no!* From my research and from the numerous offenders I have spoken with, I am convinced that any punishment the offender might receive as a result of a crime is not a deterrent to such violent acts. Teens just don't think about the consequences when committing or even planning their crimes. Many of these young men and women are so depressed they don't care if they live or die, let alone spend a lifetime behind bars. Some even welcome a death sentence.

Since, in my opinion, legal discipline does not necessarily help in preventing crime, what's the point in making criminals pay? I believe that prison sentences should be used to mainly focus on the rehabilitation of the offender and to keep society safe from dangerous criminals. Let's look at some general guidelines and penalties our country's justice system is appropriating for teenage offenders.

Twenty or thirty years ago, there was no minimum age for a teen to be tried as an adult in a court of law. If a thirteen-year-old boy committed murder, he would be locked up in a juvenile facility until his eighteenth or twenty-first birthday, at which time he would be released into society. As the years went by and it was obvious that young adults were becoming increasingly violent, things in the legal world began to change. The laws changed in favor of trying, convicting, and sentencing young people as adults. Because of such punishment reform, violent teenagers can now spend time in an adult prison well before their eighteenth birthdays.

Currently the laws vary by state as to the minimum age a child can be tried and convicted as an adult, but the average is between thirteen and fifteen years old. While I think the sentence should depend on the crime, I do not feel that kids younger than thirteen should face an adult trial and adult punishment. Instead, they should be locked up in a youth facility and given the proper programs and counseling to have the best chance at rehabilitation. This way, upon being released on their eighteenth or twenty-first birthdays, they have a realistic and viable chance to live a law-abiding and productive life on the outside. If they don't respond to treatment—and this should be carefully evaluated—then they should be sent away to an adult facility to serve a lengthy sentence.

THE DEATH PENALTY

I agree with the United States Justice Department that juveniles, ages seventeen and younger, should not face the death penalty. Even though these individuals can commit adult crimes, they are still kids and have not yet reached full maturity, especially in their brain functions. According to numerous studies conducted between 1999 and 2004 on the juvenile brain—particularly by Dr. Jay Giedd, a child psychiatrist and chief of the brain-imaging unit at NIMH—this vital organ is basically developing until people reach roughly the age of twenty-five. UCLA brain researcher Paul Thompson concluded, "We found that the frontal lobes were the last to develop. These brain regions control inhibition, rash actions, rage and anger."[2] This portion of the brain also controls decision making, risk perception, and impulse control.

Steven Drizin, a Northwestern University law professor who helped create one of the legal briefs the Supreme Court used in making their decision that minors not face the death penalty, said, "While a fourteen or seventeen year old knows the difference between right and wrong, they don't have the same abilities to control their behaviors and assess risks the way adults do."[3]

As a result of these fascinating medical findings, in March 2005 the Supreme Court ruled that imposing the death penalty on juveniles is cruel and unusual punishment. As of today no person under the age of eighteen at the time of their crime can be put to death. The maximum sentence a convicted teen offender can be given is life without parole, which is quite frankly a death sentence inside a state prison.[4]

Before this high court decision, numerous teens had been executed in America—approximately 365.[5] Their crimes ranged from attempted rape to robbery to murder. A majority of these teens were male and most of them were African-American. Before 1900, methods of execution included the firing squad, electrocution, and hanging. After 1900, most teens were killed by hanging, electrocution, and later, the gas chamber and lethal injection.

Michael Kelleher, in his book *When Good Kids Kill,* said that corporal punishment for young people dates back to the seventeenth century.[6] In 1624, for example, sixteen-year-old Thomas Graunger was hanged. The youngest person executed in the United States since 1900 was ten-year-old James Arcene. He was hanged in Arkansas in 1885 for murder and robbery. Since the beginning of the twentieth century, the youngest person legally executed in the United States was thirteen-year-old Fortune Ferguson Jr., who was put to death for raping an eight-year-old girl.

THE LACK OF CONSISTENCY

Another major concern is the lack of consistency in our justice system. Some teenagers who have killed multiple victims are either free today or serving minimum sentences; others were simply at the wrong place at the wrong time and didn't commit the murders themselves, but are still serving life sentences. I will illustrate this inconsistency by offering examples of some brutal crimes with surprisingly little consequences, and some less-violent incidences that have resulted in lengthy and what I would consider unfair penalties.

HE GOT WHAT?

This case involves a minor who committed a terrible crime and was basically given a slap on the wrist as a penalty. I have previously talked about fourteen-year-old Cody Posey, who lived with his family at a New Mexico ranch owned by ABC reporter Sam Donaldson. This boy shot and killed his entire family in response to the physical and mental abuse he endured from his father. Along with killing his dad, Cody killed his stepmother, by shooting her twice in the head, and his stepsister, whom he shot twice in the face. Cody claimed he shot his stepmother because she was mean to him, and that he murdered his stepsister to eliminate any witnesses. He also tried to cover up the crime by burying the bodies, which were found two days later by workers at Sam Donaldson's ranch.

What punishment did this young man receive for his triple murder? He was ordered to a juvenile facility until his twenty-first birthday, and at the time, it was possible for him to serve as little as forty days. Not only did Cody murder three people, but he also had spent the next two days carrying on and having fun as if nothing had happened. Doesn't there seem to be a lack of common sense and reasonable judgment in the level of punishment Cody received?

OBVIOUS INJUSTICE

We know some cases of teen killers serving lengthy sentences who do not seem to warrant such severe penalty. In Florida in 1992, fourteen-year-old Timothy Kane was at a friend's house, playing video games on Super Bowl Sunday, when four of his older friends decided to burglarize a neighbor's home. Not wanting to stay behind and be left out, Timothy decided to tag along.

The five youths rode their bikes to their target's home and even fed some ducks along the way. Two of the boys took off before the crime, but Timothy followed nineteen-year-old Alvin Morton and seventeen-year-old Bobby Garner into the house. In a later interview, Timothy said, "This is the decision that shaped my life since."[7]

The group had assumed the home would be vacant, so they were surprised to find the homeowner, seventy-five-year-old Madeline Weisser, and her son present. Court testimony revealed that Timothy hid behind the dining room table as the other two teens went ballistic. Alvin, described by prosecutors as a sociopath, shot and killed the man in the back of the neck while he begged for his life. He then tried to shoot the elderly woman, but his gun jammed. Using a dull knife, Alvin stabbed her in the neck. Because it was so dull, Alvin had to step on the weapon to wedge it deep into her neck, almost resulting in a decapitation. Prosecutor Robert W. Attridge said, "I firmly believe what they were trying to do was take the head as a kind of souvenir."[8]

The boys sliced off the male victim's pinkie finger, which they later paraded around to friends. Alvin was given a death sentence, and Bobby was sentenced to life without parole. I can understand and definitely approve of these sentences. But what about Timothy? He was sentenced to life without parole for twenty-five years for simply hiding behind a dining room table. If he had committed his crime after 1995, however, it would have been worse. He would have had absolutely no chance of parole. Timothy said, "I witnessed two people die. I regret that every day of my life, being any part of that and seeing that."[9] He is not optimistic he will ever be released.

Florida's Tim Kane, who at the age of fourteen had the unfortunate luck to be present while his friends committed a heinous double murder in Florida on Super Bowl Sunday in 1992.

Did this young man, who did not actively participate in this heinous crime, deserve the kind of punishment he received? I certainly don't think so! Should he serve some hard time for tagging along with his buddies and not making an effort to stop the crime? Absolutely! But I think a life sentence is too extreme.

Another case has to do with a suburban gang from Florida called "the Lords of Chaos." This particular group has garnered a ton of media attention. Of most interest to me are not necessarily the facts of the crime but the senseless punishment of the offenders. In 1996, eighteen-year-olds Kevin Don Foster, Derek Shields, and Christopher Black, and seventeen-year-old Peter Magnotti were members of this gang and committed a string of petty crimes, including vandalism and robbery.

As they wreaked havoc in the city of Fort Myers, their crime spree took a more violent twist when they shot and killed a music teacher who worked at the high school. The four young vandals attempted to break the windows at the high school and were caught by the school's music teacher. Outraged, he told the young men that they would all be suspended the following Monday. The boys were immediately sent home.

The threat did not sit well with the gang's ringleader, Kevin Foster. Kevin

(**left**) *Prison photo of Kevin Foster, who shot and killed a music teacher at the front door of the teacher's home. The teacher had caught Kevin and his friends vandalizing the school earlier that night.*

(**center**) *Prison photo of Derek Shields, who was caught hanging with the wrong crowd one night and was given a life sentence. A codefendant, Kevin Foster, shot and killed a music teacher.*

(**right**) *Christopher Black, who is serving a life sentence for hanging with the wrong crowd and being present during the shooting death of a music teacher at his high school.*

came from a family who bought, sold, and used guns. They owned a pawn-shop that contained a wide collection of weapons Kevin had easy access to. He hatched a devious plan and informed the rest of the gang members that they would be killing the music teacher to avoid suspension from school. The others initially refused to participate in the psychotic plan, but Kevin threatened them with violence if they did not follow through. In fear of their lives, the three boys felt they had no other choice but to comply with Kevin's demands.

From what I understand, Derek rang the doorbell of the teacher's home, and Christopher and Peter waited in the car. When the door opened, Kevin shot the man one time at point-blank range with a 12-gauge shotgun, instantly killing him. They fled the scene but were arrested soon afterward. All were charged with first degree murder even though Kevin was the shooter, the killer, and the one who planned the crime. Derek, who had a student scholarship, was given a life sentence without parole for ringing the doorbell and running off. Christopher, an honor student, was given the same sentence for being the getaway driver. Peter, a genius and a talented artist, was sent to jail for thirty-two years for sitting in a car. Kevin, perhaps the only offender with a reasonable sentence, was given the death penalty. Can you see the lack of logic here? Each person's role in this crime was different, but their punishments were almost equal.

When I asked Christopher what he believed his punishment should have been, he thought for a moment and answered:

> I believe, and maybe not rightly so, that I should have spent a day in prison for every day I'd spent free. Namely, eighteen years and twenty days. It doesn't seem like much, but trust me, it feels like forever. To be followed by an equal period of probation, during which I would be required to make financial restitutions to those of which I destroyed or damaged or stole property from, in conjunction with educating young people as to my crime, my crime's results, my time in prison, and what they can do to avoid my fate. I would do so until my probation was completed. The sentence I received was life in prison without the possibility of parole.

WHAT IS APPROPRIATE?

What kind of punishment should teen killers face? In my opinion, it must be a serious and severe penalty—excluding execution—that also offers a plan for rehabilitation and a chance for redemption. I feel teens should have the chance to turn their lives around and have the opportunity to become positively contributing members of society. For those who do not take these proper steps and, instead, maintain a life of violence and crime, they should remain locked up for the remainder of their natural lives. Most important, we need to shift our efforts from warehousing and punishing kids to educating and rehabilitating them, with the hope of preventing violent crime. This benefits everyone and, hopefully in the long run, will save innocent lives.

FOR MORE INFORMATION ON TEEN MURDER
AND THE CASES COVERED IN THIS BOOK,
LOG ON TO WWW.PHILCHALMERS.COM.
DON'T MISS PHIL'S BOOK,
THE ENCYCLOPEDIA OF TEEN KILLERS.

EIGHT

MY SPACE:
LIFE IN PRISON AS A TEEN

Prison is a Vietnam or a strait jacket. What I mean is you'll
either live day to day surrounded by potential ambushes and
booby traps, or you'll live day to day locked into one room left
to your own devices.

—TODD RIZZO,
teen killer, on death row in a Connecticut prison

Luke Woodham said, "It is a sad day when you have to try to convince
people that a place [prison] as bad as this is really bad." Luke lives in a six-
by-ten prison cell at the Mississippi State Penitentiary, the oldest prison and
the only maximum security prison in the state. He is allowed three five-
minute showers a week, and the only time he can leave his cell is to take a
shower or go to the prison yard. He spends about an hour each weekday
outside in the yard that is divided into three separate pens, smaller gated
areas within the yard. These were built because of the massive number of
fights that erupted in the open yard. The pens were the only option to keep
the prisoners from killing each other.

Without access to TV or the radio, Luke's day consists of waking up,
reading the Bible and praying, eating breakfast, studying, eating lunch,
reading, writing letters, eating supper, reading the Bible, and going to sleep.
He will continue this monotonous routine for the rest of his life. Luke is
only allowed a limited amount of reading material, which is closely moni-
tored. During the cold winters the prison remains minimally heated, and

during the summer months there is no air conditioning. Luke washes his dirty clothes in the sink or toilet so no one will steal them. He is allowed visits from his family once a month and the interaction is made possible by a telephone and a Plexiglas window divider. For some reason, the state of Mississippi and the Mississippi State Penitentiary will not allow Luke to do any interviews that would help other wayward teens avoid a path of destruction. They also have banned me from entering the prison, which is strange since the purpose of my organization is to stop teen murders.

Luke wrote:

I was given three life sentences and one hundred forty years and unless God says otherwise, this is how I will spend my life until the day that I die. The worst part is the loneliness. You are completely alone. There are other people around you, but none live with you. You never get to see your family *ever again*, except through plexiglass. All you are stuck with for company is your dead dreams, your bad memories, and the pain of how life might have been if you had only taken another course in life. Those are the only things that I have left and all that I will own until I die and I am only twenty-three.

Many people have asked me, "What is prison really like?" The truth is that I have never spent any time locked up. While I cannot give a personal account, I can share the experiences of the many offenders I know who are spending the rest of their lives behind bars.

As is the case of the juvenile justice system, there is no consistency within the prison system, so these facilities vary from state to state. There are different levels of prisons, from maximum security prisons that house killers, rapists, and violent offenders, to minimum security prisons that are a step up from a summer camp. Prison is very bad for some, and for others it is more than bearable. Some prisons are pure hellholes, and others seem to be more civilized. Some prisons have very strict rules, and others grant inmates a lot of freedom. Nonetheless, being locked up is never a good place to be. The reality is that at any given moment you could be seriously hurt, raped, or even killed.

Prison in America and around the world has moved from a place of rehabilitation to a place of punishment. Many believe that is the way it should be, and perhaps on some level they are right. My view, however, is that during the time offenders are being punished, we should also do our best to rehabilitate them. The goal of the criminal justice system, for those in prison who have a possibility of parole, should be to reform them so they can ultimately make a positive contribution to society.

I'm sure you are asking the questions, but how on earth do we rehabilitate offenders? and is it even possible? Those are very meaningful questions, and rehabilitation is a very controversial subject. I do believe, however, that many offenders can be rehabilitated. I am confident that with effective recovery programs, psychological counseling, and spiritual guidance, men and women can turn their lives around for the better. Time and time again, I have personally watched offenders switch gears, get help, and lead successful lives.

When it comes to violent criminals like serial rapists and murderers, I have a different opinion. These types of offenders are definitely tougher to rehabilitate. For many of them it may be impossible because of the enormous depth of the violence associated with their crimes. Once a person has engaged in the combination of sex and murder, the strong inner drive that caused him to commit the crime may likely provoke him to do it again. There needs to be an extreme amount of caution exerted when considering such a person's release into regular society.

Crimes involving murder and rape are much different from offenses like drunk driving or drug use. There is also a considerable difference between a sexual predator who sexually assaults and murders children and a high school boy who is being bullied and kills his tormenter. Both crimes are heinous, yes, but the underlying motivations and behaviors that contribute to the crime vary to greater and lesser degrees.

There are those criminals who simply refuse to change and want to continue their lifestyle of violence, rape, and murder. Rehabilitation is pretty impossible, so there seems to be no other option than to permanently house them in a facility that keeps the public safe from them and provides humane living conditions.

IN THEIR OWN WORDS

I have asked a handful of inmates what prison is really like, especially for a teenager, and would like to present some of those stories to give you a better idea of what happens behind bars.

In chapter 4, I talked about Austin Addison—the New York teen who shot and killed another teen over a jacket. He had this to say about prison:

> Prison is one big hellhole . . . it's no fun having officers looking into your anus after every visit, in fact it's dehumanizing and degrading . . . you'll find yourself fighting, stabbing or getting stabbed to hold yourself down . . . prison is another form of a slave plantation . . . Most kids come in now are scared and end up joining a gang or become Muslim for protection, and those who don't and are weak end up as prey.

Brian Houchin, the sixteen-year-old bank robber from Indiana, who was mentioned in the last chapter, gave me his description:

> Prison—it's horrible! It's a mental torture . . . you name it, it's here. I've seen it: rape, murder, stabbings, and guys being burned alive. It is a deadly place full of anger, pain, frustration, hate, darkness, dreams are nightmares and hope is gone. There are killers, rapists, thieves and molesters—every dreg from society, the undesirables. You have to watch your back constantly. Factor in all of the mental patients who are subject to snap and start stabbing guys at random for no reason . . . To the administration, you are just a slab of meat that helps to pull in a larger budget for them to get bigger kickbacks. The health care system is a joke. It is a place of punishment—rehabilitation is something you have to get yourself . . . It isn't something they encourage. The rules of the jungle apply—the strong overpower the weak. Nothing is cool about this. There is no fame, there is no glory to be had, and you don't get any "props" for coming to the joint. The young are taken advantage of at every given chance.

Prison photo of Robin Robinson, one of the very first school shooters, who shot his principal in Alabama in 1978. He later beat an ex-police officer to death in a botched robbery attempt and was given a very lengthy sentence.

I introduced Robin Robinson in the first chapter as one of the earliest school shooters in America. He was also involved in a botched robbery that resulted in the fatal beating of a former police officer. Robin has spent many years locked up in state prisons. He is now serving a thirty-year sentence in an Alabama institution. Robin told me about his ordeal behind bars:

Prison is hell. I have had to stab a guy, and I've also been stabbed. Since being in prison from the age of sixteen, I've had to deal with cold, hard criminals, many off of death row, with life without parole and life sentences, including murderers, rapers, and child molesters. I spent my first ten years in two maximum security facilities, and I've seen guys raped, robbed, and murdered for nothing. I've seen guys cut and stabbed for something that could have easily been avoided. I stabbed a guy simply because I felt that he disrespected me, and I was stabbed in another incident years later about some prison-made alcohol in a fight that nearly cost me my life. I was stabbed in the side with my own prison-made knife that I was intending to use to kill another inmate.

Robin told me about the code of conduct in prison:

In prison you live by a false code of conduct. We call it the "convict code," where you mind your own business, you keep others out of your business, and you don't "snitch" or let anyone disrespect you. I've seen more guys lose their lives and freedom trying to uphold this false code more than anything else. I've seen guys with a few years left end up with life, life without parole, or on death row trying to enforce this code. You're subject to lose your life any minute or moment in prison . . . prison also promotes homosexuality and masturbation. After prison, many guys are not equipped to function in society, and many become "institutionalized." They end up returning to prison time and time again.

Of the culture behind bars Robin said:

Prison is filled with young, poor, white, and black gang members. Hip-hop and rap is their culture and language. Many of them cannot read or write but can quote Jay-Z, Tupac, 50 Cent, and Eminem verbatim . . . drugs and fast cash is all they want and dream about. The young whites here are victims of crystal meth, and the young blacks are victims of crack and cocaine . . . Both are victims of the system that exploits us from A to Z. Probation officers, lawyers, police, judges, district attorneys, prisons, guards, wardens, parole officers, etc., all exploit inmates. Even the phone services, canteen, and health care system exploit inmates. In my opinion, the prison system is a sham. They want us to stay in prison and come back. Many inmates have served more time than their crimes warrant.

He explained what happens when a person gets sick in prison: "If you get sick, you sign up for treatment, pay for treatment, and wait on a doctor that may or may not decide to see you. I can't count the number of guys that have been killed or died from various illnesses over the years."

Robin continued to relate some of the horrible aspects of being isolated from the real world: "I can't count the number of guys I have seen raped over the years. I can't count the number that have lost their mothers or fathers, grandmothers and grandfathers, and other loved ones and cannot attend their funerals. I can't count the number of guys I've seen go crazy or have to be admitted to mental treatment. Not to mention the number that committed suicide."

He ended his description of life as an inmate by saying, "I eat when they feed me, I sleep when they say I can sleep, I don't own or control anything. Not even my own body! I'm the property of the Alabama State Department of Corrections, a modern-day slave. I go when and where they say I go, and I do what they say I am supposed to do."

Since being locked up Robin has turned his life around, gotten involved in recovery and spiritual programs, and is preparing for his upcoming release. He is confident he will never return to prison and is looking forward to leading a productive life outside the Alabama prison gates.

Gena Lawson was involved in a stabbing outside a high school in Pensacola, Florida. She was bullied at school by two girls and retaliated against them one day in self-defense. She was convicted of homicide, sentenced to twenty years in prison, and is now serving her sentence in Lowell, Florida. In 2000, while incarcerated, Gena was diagnosed with the disease lupus, or SLE. She reflected, "It's been a never-ending battle for my life ever since. I've experienced much neglect and indifferent treatment from the Department of Corrections."

In 2003, she was let out on what is called "medical clemency." This simply means she was sent home to die because she was not deemed to be a threat to society. Once she started to recover from her illness, however, she was returned to complete her prison term and, at that time, had thirteen more years to go.

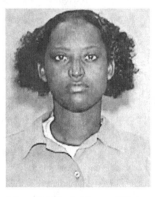

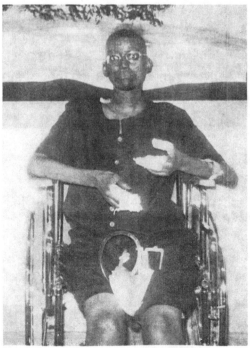

(above) *Prison photo of Gena Lawson, who stabbed two sisters after school in Florida because they were threatening and bullying her. One survived, the other died.*

(right) *Gena Lawson suffered from lupus in prison and was released to die, only to recover and be sent back to serve her lengthy sentence.*

What is a women's prison like in Florida? Gena explained:

I describe prison as being a place where one can learn how to commit more crimes, practice perverse sexual behavior, and completely disregard the law and morality. I think it's horrible . . . All I do is sit around and watch the officers harass and demean the other inmates. I am not exempt from this behavior. It happens to me quite often.

She continued:

The food is horrendous—watered down, cold, tasteless, and barely edible. Even if you wanted to eat the food it would be a waste of time because the portions are so small you would still be as hungry as you were before you ate it. The majority of the time you are yelled at and treated like animals by the officers. If you have a lengthy sentence, furthering your education is not an option . . . People on the outside have the misconception that prison is like a vacation, college, or something other than what it really is . . . Prison is a place of survival and only the strong survive.

Gena specifically pleads with young girls who will listen to her message:

You do not want to come here. Besides hell, this is not a place you want to be. Prison is a place full of crime, violence, loneliness, despair, and believe it or not, peer pressure. Some of the things that happen to kids who come here are unspeakable. I was only sixteen when I came to prison and fortunately, I was never raped. It has happened to several young girls that I knew. Young girls are often conned, raped, and taken advantage of . . . Crime doesn't pay. The only thing it leads to is heartache and a ruined life. Communicate with your parents. Laws were established for our safety as well as our well-being. There is no excuse or reason to break them. Life is precious and time lost can never be regained.

Ron Ward was involved in a stabbing at a drug house in Arkansas when he was only fifteen years old. He told me he was innocent of the stabbing and was simply at the wrong place at the wrong time. Ron was sentenced to death row for his crime. His sentence had been commuted to life in prison with no chance of parole though, as previously mentioned, he died in prison from cancer.

Ron was sent to death row in an adult prison and gave an eye-opening, firsthand account of his experience:

> I have been told what to do and when to do it for twenty-four years. There is no privacy in prison, and you are exposed when showering and using the bathroom by other males. And yes, some of these males are all-out homosexuals. Homosexuality goes on frequently, and being in prison within a year you will see plenty of this activity and this behavior . . .
>
> Stabbings, killings, and all kinds of acts of violence I have witnessed many times, and I've also witnessed dudes that come here with six-year sentences and die in prison from stab wounds. I've also seen guys come in with a twenty-year sentence and end up with life without parole for a murder committed in prison. I've seen gruesome beatings that prison officials inflict upon troublesome prisoners, and prison officials sometime[s] kill the prisoner and put the blame on someone else.

Ron lamented, "I matured as a responsible adult in prison, and now that I'm looking back on my life I see that I have experienced misery and pain for most of my life. My father and mother abandoned me before my first birthday, and my grandparents raised me from that time until my arrest at the young age of fifteen."

James Evans dated Wendy Gardner, and both lived in New York. Wendy allegedly suffered from physical abuse at the hands of her grandmother, and James wanted to put an end to it. He strangled the elderly woman with a kite string, and the two lovers then threw her body into the trunk of a car. James, convicted of second degree murder, said that he killed to protect his girlfriend. He now understands it was a terrible mistake.

James gave me his report of life in a tough New York prison:

MY SPACE

You can't see your family when you want, and when you do see them, they are harassed by the guards and the prison . . . I have to get pat frisked on the way in to the visit, and strip searched on the way out . . . In New York it costs eight dollars to make a thirty-minute call, and all your calls must be collect. That means you may not be able to contact anyone if they don't accept collect calls . . . for some people, even family and friends turn their backs on them over time. Being locked in a six by eight cell is very trying on a person.

Todd Rizzo, whose story is shared in chapter 4, is a very intelligent individual and, in my opinion, probably the most articulate offender I know in expressing himself and describing the different aspects of his crime. Todd was obsessed with horror movies and serial killers from a young age. He acted out a scene from the film *The Texas Chainsaw Massacre* on a young boy in his neighborhood, killing his victim with a sledgehammer. Todd told about living in a Connecticut state prison, including what happened during his first few days behind bars:

The first place I was brought to after the police department was the county jail . . . Everyone seemed to hate me on sight and wanted to either fight me or rape me . . . I was strip searched, and guys holler, bang, and rap all day and all night. I barely slept . . . I had to walk past other cells, and absorbed more threats and glares with added spit . . . the dude directly across from my cell aimed and pissed at me, but none got in my cell. Only splatter.

I was photographed nude because of my abdomen tattoo, but right in front of female officers . . . they kept me naked for probably forty-five minutes before showering me again with a lice rake . . . I was then sentenced to death at the age of twenty for a crime I committed at the age of eighteen. I was brought to a maximum security correctional facility, to death row . . . I lost track of how many nosy visitors I had by the close of day one, walking past my cell. From plain guards to brass to medical and mental health personnel, to the higher ups including the warden. All of them had to come see the new albino monkey at the zoo.

125

In describing his cell, he said, "It is seven by twelve feet, noticeably larger than most in the U.S. penal system but nonetheless a locked, concrete prison cell . . . there's a toilet-sink combo but both the water output and the flush have timers to prevent overflowing, since some inmates get a kick out of flooding the tier. The mirror bolted to the wall can double as a marred cookie sheet. The door is solid steel, no classic bars."

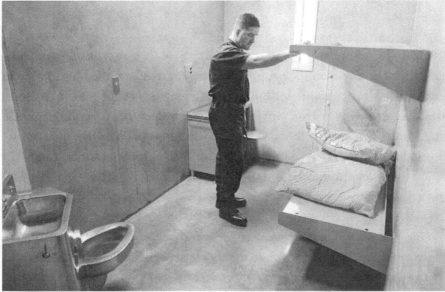

(AP Photo / Steve Miller)

A typical prison cell on death row at Northern Correctional Institution in Somers, Connecticut. This is the kind of cell Todd Rizzo resides in.

Todd's advice to today's teens who may think serving time behind bars is glamorous and cool rings a loud warning:

Prison is not a ghetto hotel. Depending on your sentence and behavior, which determines your housing and privileges, prison is a Vietnam or a strait jacket. What I mean is you'll either live day to day surrounded by potential ambushes and booby traps, or you'll live day to day locked into one room left to your own devices. It's only cool and fun when sleeping if you are granted a dream. Whether you are strong and tough, or weak and skinny, you will have to deal with a homosexual encounter. Your day will eventually come, and if you are not tough, you will be made into a bitch.

(above) *Prison photo of Tennessee school shooter Jamie Rouse, who shot and killed a teacher and a student in Lynnville, Tennessee.*

(right) *Phil visiting Tennessee school shooter Jamie Rouse. Rouse was inspired by violent music and the violent movie* Natural Born Killers.

Many offenders serving life sentences have a hope or dream that their case will be overturned, and they will one day have a chance at freedom. Sadly, this is wishful thinking for most. Yet there are those who have come to terms with their fate—the fact that they will die in prison.

Not many inmates who are locked up in prison want to admit that they have been raped or sexually violated. A few men, however, have been honest with me. One of these guys is Joseph Willey, who, at the age of sixteen, stabbed a friend to death in Polk County, Florida. Sentenced to life at the same age, Joseph was shipped off to an adult prison and had to fight to survive against seasoned, adult prisoners. When I asked Joseph if he was ever molested growing up, he told me, "I was never molested as a child, but as an adult . . . when I first entered prison at the age of sixteen."

When I asked him what he thought about young people who think prison is cool because of the hype created from the media and the hip-hop community, he responded, "I think any kid who thinks prison is cool and wouldn't mind going there is a very unintelligent individual, and should be taken to the East unit here in Florida and locked in a cell for two months. Then ask them what they think about prison." Joseph concluded, "I have had a lot of fights in prison, and a lot of them have been defending myself against sexual assault."

Jamie Rouse, one of the early school shooters, killed two people and injured another. He gave me a very descriptive account of prison life:

> Prison sucks. I wake up between 6:20 and 7:30. I go and eat a lousy breakfast. I go to work from 8:30 till 2:30. I come back to a noisy pod where there is constant chaos. There is absolutely no peace or privacy. I have to take a shower in a stall with a big open window so that anyone can watch me. Anyone can look into my cell, even if I'm using the toilet. I get locked in my cell at 9:00 at night and stay locked down until 6:20 the next morning. I'm locked down with another man and will have to live in a twelve by six cell with someone for the rest of my life. During the times I'm locked down, I have to use the toilet with another man in the cell. I have to smell him when he uses it. I have to worry about my cell being robbed while I'm at work or at the chow hall. I have to hide any fear or weakness that I might have or I will be preyed upon. I can trust no one . . .
>
> Since the first day I got here, the homosexuals have been trying to get with me. Society tends to think it's a country club here, but that is the farthest thing from the truth. The food is terrible. I sleep on a lumpy cot that has no springs. I have to stay here and watch life pass me by. I only get to hear about the stuff my family is doing. I'm no longer a part of their lives. Instead, I only get to see the terrible things of prison. I know young guys who have been forced to commit homosexual acts. Some have been turned into "punks," guys who act like women. If you think all this is cool, then you'll love prison.

A PRISONER'S RIGHTS

As I've mentioned before, I believe it is important to provide those who want help the necessary programs for rehabilitation—things like continuing education, drug or alcohol treatment, and counseling. I also believe it is important to supply inmates with jobs—to allow them to contribute to society as they earn money for the essentials they might need while incarcerated. After communicating with inmates all over the country, I learned that recreation and sports activities also help to keep them busy while doing something constructive.

While I see no problem with inmates owning televisions or listening devices if they purchase the items themselves, I do have issues with them watching or listening to violent or pornographic entertainment. The truth is, many of these people continue to feed their hate, violence, and sexual perversion with material that some prisons permit them to purchase and use for entertainment. Pornography is one of these items.

Several of the inmates I have spoken to informed me that they have the opportunity to buy and read porn. Some of them have even asked me to purchase it for them, which, of course, I declined. Offenders convicted of violent and sexually deviant crimes should not have access to violent or pornographic media. Their violent tendencies and behaviors would be aggravated and their chances of being rehabilitated greatly diminished.

Daniel LaPlante is one such example. In 1987, at age seventeen, he killed a woman in Townsend, Massachusetts, in what I consider to be one of the most shocking murders I have come across in my research. He stripped a pregnant mother, raped her, and shot her to death in the head. Daniel then drowned her two children in two separate bathtubs. He was given a life sentence with no parole, which I believe was warranted because of the severity of his crime.

I recently read that this young man had sued the prison system and the state of Massachusetts. You won't believe why! Daniel complained that the pornography he received by mail was being withheld. A Boston law firm, Palmer & Dodge, took his case pro bono and argued before a U.S. District Court judge that Daniel's civil rights were being violated. The judge agreed and mandated that the prison stop withholding his sexually explicit mail.

The defense law firm, who had originally agreed to take on Daniel's case for free, submitted a bill to the court for $125,000 for their time and efforts.

The judge approved payment of $99,981 and ordered that the state of Massachusetts foot the legal bill. *Boston Globe* writer Brian McGrory summed up this insane injustice best in his September 16, 2005, article: "In short, LaPlante gets top-shelf legal representation. Palmer & Dodge gets another hundred grand. And as too often happens, state taxpayers get nothing more than the bill."[1]

The bottom line concerning prison is that it is a terrible place to spend any length of time. Being locked up in a building and losing your freedom is punishment in itself; and having a relatively dangerous environment filled with violent assaults, rape, and murder thrown into that mix just makes things worse. It's especially difficult for some teenagers who are locked up with adult offenders. Many are easy prey, just like in a jungle, and eventually will be taken advantage of, sexually assaulted, and possibly killed. Rest assured, prisons are not country clubs. They are living nightmares.

FOR MORE INFORMATION ON TEEN MURDER AND THE CASES COVERED IN THIS BOOK, LOG ON TO WWW.PHILCHALMERS.COM. DON'T MISS PHIL'S BOOK, *THE ENCYCLOPEDIA OF TEEN KILLERS.*

NINE

Teens and the Triangle: A Look at the Homicidal Triad

> I found a dog and cut it open just to see what the insides
> looked like, and for some reason I thought it would be a fun
> prank to stick the head on a stake and set it out in the woods.

> **—Jeffrey Dahmer,**
> serial killer, on the beginning of his animal abuse

Luke Woodham wrote in his personal journals: "On Saturday of last week, I made my first kill . . . The victim was a loved one. My dear dog Sparkle . . . I'll never forget the sound of her breaking under my might. I hit her so hard I knocked the fur off her neck . . . It was true beauty."[1]

As an impressionable child tightly gripped in the influential clutch of Satanist Grant Boyette, Luke obviously cared about what his "friend" thought—what or who Grant liked or didn't like. Well, Grant didn't like Luke's shih tzu–mix dog, Sparkle. The pet seemed too eager, too demanding, too pitiful. Anytime she noticed someone with food, she would—as most dogs do—excitedly jump up and down, ferociously wag her tail, and beg for some crumbs with her big, desperate eyes. It made Grant's skin crawl, so something needed to be done about it.

Grant initially responded to Sparkle's pleas for snacks by repeatedly kicking "the stupid b—." Finally, he suggested that Luke engage in the fun. As Grant's loyal and obedient sidekick, Luke submitted to his own perverse instincts. During a two-week period, the pair unrelentingly hit the dog with their fists and kicked her all over her body. Sparkle began walking with a recognizable limp.

Luke's mother and brother made an appointment for their family pet to see a veterinarian. Luke panicked. He knew any reasonable doctor could figure out what was happening to Sparkle, so he called Grant and begged for his help. Grant knew exactly what needed to be done. They would kill the dog, bury her body, and make Luke's mother believe Sparkle ran away.

The day of the murder Grant and Luke shoved the dog in a backpack and tossed her in the trunk of Grant's car. After driving to an isolated area of land that Grant's family owned, they took the petrified animal out of the bag and tortured her to death. Luke threw her body into a pond. He was a hollow being—numb and void of emotions. He didn't care about the loving relationship Sparkle and he had shared. He didn't care she was an innocent animal who wasn't capable of defending herself. He simple didn't care. Grant was convinced that if Luke hadn't killed his dog, his bottled-up anger would have caused him to go crazy. But it was too late. Luke had no emotions to do anything except kill.

Although Luke didn't participate in significant arson, he had a fascination with fire as a child. He loved watching candles flicker and would play with the flames. He got a thrill out of burning action figure toys. He became excited lighting matches and watching them burn out. He enjoyed destroying things the way he felt he was being destroyed every day. You may think these activities are innocent and "normal," but Luke's underlying motive was definitely questionable. He had a scary desire for destructive power that one day he would use to massacre innocent people.

Luke's history shows two of the three elements of the "homicidal triad"—also known as the "homicidal triangle" or the "psychopathological triad"—a combination of three childhood behaviors that many murderers, especially serial killers, exhibit in their early years. These include enuresis (bed-wetting), pyromania (setting fires), and animal torture. Expert criminologists and mental health physicians view this combination as a major danger signal in a young person's life. J. M. MacDonald first described the homicidal triad in his article

"The Threat to Kill," published in the *American Journal of Psychiatry*, and it is sometimes referred to as "the MacDonald Triad."[2] Luke did not experience bed-wetting, but to his recollection he did engage in the other two behaviors.

John Douglas, former chief of the FBI's Investigative Support Unit and an author who has interviewed hundreds of serial killers, indicated that "not every boy who displays these traits is going to grow up to be a killer, but the combination of the three was so prominent in our study subjects that we began recommending that a pattern (rather than isolated incidences) of any two of them should raise a warning flag for parents and teachers."[3] Douglas added that if a person displays two of the three traits, he or she has "the beginnings of a sociopathic behavior that isn't likely to correct itself on its own. This is unlikely to be a phase."

One of my favorite crime writers and criminal profilers, Pat Brown, explained the homicidal triad in her book *Killing for Sport*:

> When children feel like they have no control over their environment, behavioral problems tend to crop up. As they struggle to gain some kind of power over their lives and others in it, they often resort to anti-social behaviors . . . An eight-year-old Mike DeBardeleben would have been hard pressed to arrange an appointment with a realtor at a vacant house as a prospective homebuyer (setting up his ruse to rape and kill); but he sure as heck could set the neighbor's tool shed on fire.[4]

Teen killer Todd Rizzo's story best illustrates the homicidal triad. In 1997, Todd was an eighteen-year-old young man living in Connecticut, who as a child often dreamed of becoming a serial killer. When he finally decided it was time to kill, he lured a thirteen-year-old boy into the woods behind his house, with the promise of looking for snakes. When the boy wasn't looking, Todd hit him over the head with a sledgehammer thirteen times while the victim tearfully begged for his life.

Todd, an articulate and well-spoken man, now seems genuinely remorseful for his actions. He shared with me his thoughts about his personal triad experience:

It bothers me to admit that there is such a thing as tormenting animals, setting fires, and wetting the bed, used by law enforcement to profile would-be serial killers. It also bothers me that I am guilty of all three. As much as I loved all the pets we had, I often hurt them but always apologized and consoled them afterwards, if that makes any sense. I've whipped my dog for no good reason and choked my cats. I also put them in the microwave and freezer, and touched a match to their whiskers. My pet rats were tormented worst.

I set small fires, not arson range, mind you. Just blazes in the basement or backyard, basically to watch certain toys burn and melt. I'd light a piece of paper amazed at the char and curl. Two times only did I set dangerous fires, but still not arson range.

I wet the bed from birth to about the tenth grade. This latter part I'm most ashamed of. I know it was out of my control but sometimes I let it happen when I could easily have up and walked to the toilet. Bed-wetting handicapped my childhood. I think my bladder was the arch-bully of my past. On top of all three admissions, I grew up dreaming of being a serial killer. Jeffrey Dahmer was my idol.

Enuresis (Bed-Wetting)

About five to seven million kids in America wet the bed. Bed-wetting is most common in children in preschool and under the age of seven. Harold Schechter, a prolific author of true crime books and professor of American Literature and Culture at Queens College, suggested that if this habit persists beyond the age of twelve, it might signify a deeper pathology. The FBI reported that 60 percent of sexually related murderers and serial killers suffered with bed-wetting in their adolescent years. While many teen killers and those who have committed violent crimes have struggled with bed-wetting, many of them are too embarrassed to talk about it, let alone admit to it.

Arthur Shawcross, known as the "Genesee River Killer," was a cannibal killer who murdered a total of thirteen people, including prostitutes, friends, and children. He conducted his murderous rampage in upstate New York from

1988 through 1990. Shawcross had a very cruel and awful upbringing. This persistent bed-wetter allegedly was molested by an aunt, sodomized with a broom handle by his mother, and raped while in grade school.

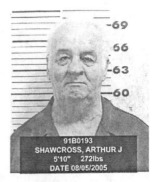

Though relatively unknown, Shawcross committed some of the most unspeakable crimes against corpses and farm animals. In an interview, Shawcross recounted the murder of a family friend and said, "I was one sick person."[5] Showercross has since died in prison from natural causes.

Serial killer Arthur "the Genesee River Killer" Shawcross was a cannibal killer who murdered a total of thirteen people including prostitutes, friends, and children. Growing up, he wet his bed late in life and allegedly was molested by his mother.

Alton Coleman wet his pants so much that his friends nicknamed him "Pissy." In 1984, he went on a six-state killing spree and murdered eight people ranging in ages from seven to seventy-seven. Coleman's methods of murder included shooting, stabbing, and strangulation. He committed other crimes, including rape and armed robbery. He was executed in 2002.

Sixteen-year-old Joseph Willey, while drunk, participated in homosexual sex with a friend. Humiliated by the situation when he regained sobriety, he decided the only thing that would make him feel right was to kill his friend. Joseph revealed some specifics of the crime to me: "I came up behind Eddie and stabbed him in the back, he jumped up and turned around, and when he did, I stabbed him again in the stomach. We both fell and I held him down until he stopped moving . . . I actually felt satisfaction, like this was the answer to all of my problems and anger. I actually felt more alive than ever."

Joseph told me, "I did wet the bed growing up until I was about twelve." He also said that he "was always game for hurting others" and was about ten years old when he thought about burning down his house while his family was inside.

Pyromania (Setting Fires)

Many children, teenagers, and young adults are intrigued or fascinated with fire. Young kids especially are frequently caught playing with matches, lighters, or stoves. While often this behavior can be linked to simple curiosity or mischief, a growing obsession with fire can lead to violent and destructive conduct.

Pyromania is an interesting phenomenon. The fire starter performs this injurious misdeed as an act of revenge or destruction, and it also allows the fire-starter to have control over or manipulate the police and other rescue personnel. Setting fires can also be considered a sexual crime because it allows the criminal to undergo a sexual rush, similar to what a sexual offender feels when he rapes his victims. Harold Schechter said, "Serial murderers who enjoy starting fires do so for the same reason they love to torture and kill. It turns them on."[6] Since most serial killers don't think of humans as more than objects, it's an easy jump from setting fires to killing people.

One of the first FBI criminal profilers, John Douglas, exposed another facet to arson: "Arson is often an attempt to gain control and power and attain a feeling of success in their lives. Look at the people an arsonist gets to manipulate and control: the victims of the fire, firefighters, police and other figures of authority, the media, and even the community in general."[7]

In 1976, David "Son of Sam" Berkowitz tyrannized the Bronx area of New York at night. During the day he sorted letters at a United States Post Office. When he was younger, Berkowitz's friends called him "Pyro" due to his fondness for setting fires. He is reported to have started more than two thousand fires throughout the state. Berkowitz's writings revealed he would start them in trash cans or vacant lots, mostly in Queens and Brooklyn, and then watch as fire departments frantically responded to the calls.

Berkowitz began his wave of murder in 1976 and targeted young women with dark hair. Many of his victims were shot as they sat in parked cars with their boyfriends. Berkowitz bragged to authorities, "I only shot pretty girls."[8] By the time he was arrested, six people were dead and several others were critically and permanently injured.

David told me exclusively that he believes that Satanism and the occult were the reasons for his crime spree, but there were signs of trouble ahead when he was a youngster. He used to hide in dark closets or under a bed for hours when he was a small child. He also participated in a large amount of vandalism, which included arson. And he had an early fascination with the occult. The murders occurred when he was involved in a devil-worshipping group in New York. He also told me there were no dogs speaking to him, but instead that was a story made up by his legal team. The "Sam" in the "Son of Sam" he told police about was "Samhain," the god of the Druids, who demanded human sacrifices.

> I was at one time a devil worshipper. I made the mistake of getting involved with a group of people who were into witchcraft. I also had a hard time growing up, and for whatever reason, I was not truly able to open up to my adoptive parents. I was unable to express my anger and other emotions in constructive ways. I was fascinated with movies and stories with occult themes, and I read the Satanic Bible. Since I was a child I had a craving for darkness. I have no interest in these things anymore. I have been a Christian now for 29 years, and my life changed for good in 1987.

Since his conviction and while in prison, Berkowitz has become a born-again Christian and changed his grisly nickname to "Son of Hope." He has accepted the fact that he will spend the rest of his days behind bars. Now Berkowitz spends his time studying the Bible and helping other inmates deal with physical challenges.

Prison photo of former serial killer turned born-again Christian David "Son of Sam" Berkowitz.

Another serial killer, Carlton Gary, burned down a grocery store as a teenager. Known as the "Stocking Strangler," Gary killed older, white women, at least eight in total during the 1970s. He was convicted of three of these murders and sentenced to death in a Georgia prison. Gary, known for his charm, was so slick that he even dated a deputy sheriff while he was selling drugs and murdering women.

The following are other serial killers associated with a fascination with fire.

New Jersey serial killer Joseph Kallinger wrote, "I love the excitement of the power fire gives me . . . the mental image is greater than sex."[9]

Arthur Shawcross started a string of fires, one of which blazed at the paper factory where he worked and resulted in more than $250,000 in damage.

Thrill killer George Adorno set his sister on fire when he was only four years old.

At the age of eleven, Carl Panzram caused more than $100,000 in damage when he set fire to a reformatory he was locked up in.

In 1997 in New Jersey, eighteen-year-old Thomas Koskovich, along with a seventeen-year-old accomplice, ordered a pizza. When the delivery guy came to the door, they shot the man to death. While Thomas repeatedly denied that he was the shooter, investigators pointed to his guilt and also ascribed him as a thrill killer. In our interview, Thomas chronicled his fascination with fire: "I did play with fire a little bit. I set a trailer in my backyard on fire, pretending I was a fireman and was going to put it out, but I couldn't, and the fire department was called. I would build small houses for action figures, then light them on fire and try to rescue them."

Rod Matthews, who beat a fifteen-year-old boy to death with a baseball bat in 1986 and took friends to see the corpse after the crime, admitted his obsession with fire to police.

Another teen killer I interviewed, Dale Stewart, told me about his interest in fire as a child. Dale, who shot and killed a boy riding on a bicycle in Minnesota, said, "The only thing I did was play with fire. I would set plastic and paper on fire and watch it burn. I remember one time I was playing with matches and set the carpet in my room on fire."

Austin Addison, the New York teen who shot and killed another teen over his jacket, informed me that he took "great pleasure out of seeing and setting fires."

ANIMAL TORTURE

There is a curious form of animal torture that some of you reading this book probably exercised as a child. These are things like removing the wings of a fly; plucking off the legs of a spider; burning an insect on the sidewalk using a magnifying glass; or poking, prodding, and jabbing the family pet. Relatively harmless, right? Well, I agree. But we must use the same level of caution and awareness as with the former activities of bed-wetting and playing with fire. Animal torture can become more than just playful behavior; it can become vicious, perverse, and deadly. A child who severely tortures or has sex with an animal, otherwise known as bestiality, is exhibiting serious signs of psychological, mental, and emotional problems.

Harold Schechter differentiated between the simple curiosities of children and more troubling behavior: "Lots of little boys who enjoy pulling the wings off of flies grow up to be lawyers or dentists. The sadistic behavior of budding serial killers is something else entirely. After all, it's one thing to chop an earthworm in two because you want to watch the separate halves squirm; it's quite another to eviscerate your neighbor's pet kitten because you enjoy listening to its agonized howls."[10]

ASPCA therapist Dr. Stephanie LaFarge said, "Anyone who hurts animals has the potential to move on to people."[11] Most experts agree that animal sadism usually doesn't stop at animals. Many young people who act out this type of torture graduate from animals to human beings. In his book *The Serial Killer Files*, Schechter similarly warned that animal torture isn't a stage, but a rehearsal for future murderous acts on human beings.[12]

It is not unusual for serial killers to have, among other violent activities, decapitated cats, dissected dogs, and set animals on fire in their childhood.

Jeffrey Dahmer, one of the most famous modern-day serial killers, frequently performed "operations" on neighborhood cats and dogs and his goldfish pets, slashing them open to take a peek inside their bodies. He also collected roadkill and nailed live frogs to trees. Dahmer said, "I found a dog and cut it open just to see what the insides looked like, and for some reason

I thought it would be a fun prank to stick the head on a stake and set it out in the woods."[13]

British killer Dennis Nilson hanged a cat to see how long it would take to die. Serial killer Carroll Cole, also known as the "Barfly Strangler," used to choke the family dog unconscious. Murderers such as serial killer Peter Kurten regularly raped and killed animals. Albert Desalvo, "the Boston Strangler," trapped animals and shot them with a bow and arrow.

Joseph Aulisio, from Old Forge, Pennsylvania, was known around his community to abuse animals. In 1981, fifteen-year-old Joseph shot and killed two neighborhood children, ages four and eight, with a 12-gauge shotgun. He dumped their bodies in an abandoned mining pit. In the courtroom, when he was convicted at the end of his trial, Joseph turned to his family, raised a clenched fist, and advised it was "party time."[14]

Luis Ramon stalked and killed his aunt wearing a Freddy hockey mask like his favorite character from the movie Friday the 13th. Ramon told me that he set fires and killed animals growing up.

Luis Ramon was another fifteen-year-old boy who participated in animal torture. This Tennessee young man killed his aunt with a butcher knife while wearing a hockey mask, a similar prop used by the main character Jason in *Friday the 13th*. In prison Luis said that he thought his mission on earth was to be a serial killer and he therefore made a commitment to kill as many people as he possibly could. He told me that he "set fires and killed animals growing up."

Jim Hardy and Pete Roland were two teenagers who took part in the murder of a nineteen-year-old man in Missouri. They beat him to death with baseball bats, and when the barely alive victim pleaded for a reason for the beating, the two killers said it was fun. They then disposed of the dead body in a well. Jim and Pete were involved in Satanism, loved to listen to death metal music, and tortured animals while growing up.

New Jersey teen Sam Manzie had dark fantasies about raping and murdering little boys. It is reported that he engaged in animal abuse and tortured little children. Because of Sam's poor social skills, he had great difficulty making friends his own age. Consequently, he retreated in isolation to his bedroom for long hours, spending much of his time surfing the Internet and conversing with strangers in online chat rooms.

In 1996, Sam met a forty-three-year-old sexual predator, Steve Simmons, online. Their relationship eventually became sexual. Some believe the combination of this illicit affair and Sam's use of prescribed Ritalin catapulted him into acting out his violent fantasies. The following year Sam abducted and murdered a boy who came to his door selling candy and wrapping paper for his school.

Sam attempted to have sex with the child, strangled him with the cord of an alarm clock, and took photos of his body. He then stuffed his victim in a suitcase and kept it in his room until the next day, when he got rid of it in a wooded area near his home. Sam was charged with first degree murder and sentenced to seventy years in prison. In his statement of apology, his voice hauntingly echoed throughout the courtroom, "This isn't the way things should work out . . . I still can't figure out why I did what I did."

One of the first American school shooters, Brenda Spencer, introduced in chapter 1, had a history of animal abuse.

Brothers David and Bryan Freeman and their cousin Ben Birdwell, who attacked and murdered the Freeman family, had bragged to a friend about decapitating a cat and worshipping its dead body.

And Rod Ferrell, a self-proclaimed five-hundred-year-old vampire named Vesago, tormented his pet cat by throwing it down the stairs, breaking its neck.

When a child exhibits behaviors indicative of the homicidal triad, seek professional help immediately. These acts can represent symptoms of major underlying issues, like physical abuse, molestation, bullying, or sexual and violent thoughts. Many of our youth are struggling with problems, fears, and anxieties beyond their control. We need to pay more attention to them, guide them with love and wisdom, and teach them the priceless value of life. If a twelve-year-old child is a bed wetter, it does not mean he or she will turn into the next Jeffrey Dahmer, but it should serve as a caution for parents, teachers, and role models. They should do whatever it takes to help a possibly troubled child deal with his or her problems and ultimately live an emotionally healthy, balanced, and successful life.

FOR MORE INFORMATION ON TEEN MURDER
AND THE CASES COVERED IN THIS BOOK,
LOG ON TO WWW.PHILCHALMERS.COM.
DON'T MISS PHIL'S BOOK,
THE ENCYCLOPEDIA OF TEEN KILLERS.

TEN

DAHMER RIDES THE SCHOOL BUS: THE EARLY YEARS OF SERIAL KILLERS

Doing doubles is far more difficult than doing singles,
but on the other hand it also puts one in a position
to have twice as much fun.[1]

—GERARD JOHN SCHAEFER,
serial killer, talking about killing two teen girls at one time

In the thousands of conversations I have had throughout the years on the subject of teen killers, I am frequently asked about serial killers. It's obviously a fascinating topic for many.

A serial killer is a person who kills two or more people, with a cooling-off period in between the homicides. The murders are usually carried out in the same fashion, and there are generally similar characteristics shared among the victims. Many times there is a sexual element to the crime. Most historians and crime buffs agree that Jack the Ripper was the first serial killer in our modern era, while the first known serial killer in America was probably H. H. Holmes, who confessed to twenty-seven murders in the 1890s near the Chicago area.

In my studies of serial killers in their early childhood and teen years, I have found some common threads. For starters, most serial killers (approximately 90 percent of them) are white males. Many have high IQs but did not perform academically well in school. They come from highly unstable families, were abandoned by one or both parents, and grew up in an environment where physical, mental, emotional, or sexual abuse was prevalent. Seventy-five percent of serial killers come from families with a history of alcohol abuse, 50 percent come from families with a history of psychiatric problems, and 50 percent come from families with a history of sexual abuse.

At an early age serial killers take part in petty crimes, like theft or vandalism, and have an unhealthy obsession with sex, pornography, and voyeurism. Many also show signs of the homicidal triad, which includes bed-wetting, fire starting, and the abuse of animals and small children. Serial killers usually have a hard time bonding with parents, are typically described as "loners," and have few friends, if any. A majority of them spend an exorbitant amount of time daydreaming, and three-quarters of them have a chronic lying problem. Some serial killers have spent time in mental institutions or children's homes. Many of them have attempted suicide at least once.

WOULD-BE SERIAL KILLERS

In thinking about the relationship between the adult serial killer and teen killer, I have often wondered, *If teen killers had not been caught and sentenced to prison, could some of them have become adult serial killers in their later years?* I have also wondered, *How many known adult serial killers started murdering in their teens, thereby making them teen killers early in their criminal careers?* In this chapter, we will also investigate the upbringing and early lives of a few well-known serial killers and examine early warning signs that adults missed when there may still have been the possibility of getting them help.

To answer the above questions, I believe that some teen killers would have become serial killers had they not been caught, because there were certain elements to their crimes that mirrored the work of adult serial killers. There are four factors of a crime I take into consideration when making such a determination. I will provide examples of such murders later on.

- *Murders with a Sexual Connection:* This type of crime demonstrates a deeper motivation for killing than other types of crimes, for instance, a revenge killing or a murder during the commission of committing another crime. This type of crime signifies a lust-and-fantasy-driven crime that is very dangerous and hard to stop after just one kill.

- *A Close and Personal Method of Killing:* When a person kills people he knows and chooses a violent method to kill, like using a knife versus a gun, it suggests that the killer enjoys killing and will likely do it again.
- *Necrophilia: Having Sex with Dead Victims:* This is a sure sign of a psychopath and of a person who not only enjoys this act, but has some deeper influence driving him that will result in his killing again in order to experience this fantasy multiple times.
- *Psychopathic Behavior:* Many serial killers are psychopaths, individuals who are in touch with reality but simply are not bothered by the consequences of their evil actions or concerned with the well-being of others. Their apathy—and the mental disorders that are associated with psychopathic behavior—will lead them to commit multiple murders.

The next question is, how many serial killers started killing in their teenage years? We must keep in mind that it is impossible to know with certainty the exact number. Many of them do not make a habit of confessing to multiple murders. There are also others who brag about murders they never committed. It is challenging to sift through the details and uncover the truth. Let me share a few cases of serial killers whom I know began killing early.

It is a known fact that Edmund Kemper killed as a teenager, way before he transformed into a psychotic serial killer. Kemper killed his grandmother and grandfather at the age of fifteen. Fourteen-year-old Henry Lee Lucas, anxious to have his first sexual experience, strangled and buried a seventeen-year-old girl after she refused his sexual advances.

Carroll Cole, at the age of eight, drowned a boy his age at a social event near a lake. He pretended the murder was an accident. The victim teased Cole about his name, and Cole retaliated by ending the bully's life.

Ted Bundy, although he had adamantly denied it, has been accused of killing in his teen years. Many experts believe that when he was fourteen years old, he kidnapped an eight-year-old girl from her bed and murdered her.

Let's get back to the four elements of a crime that evidence serial-killer behavior. Let me detail some examples of teen killers who exhibited these dangerous signs and so could have ultimately evolved into a serial killer, as well as offer examples of adult serial-killer crimes where these factors were evidenced.

Murders with a Sexual Connection

Teens committing murders with a sexual connection isn't something new, and in fact these type of crimes took place as early as the late 1800s. In 1874, Jesse Harding Pomeroy from Boston, Massachusetts, killed two young boys and tortured six others ranging from ages four to eight. The victims were tied up, beaten, stabbed, and most had their throats and genitals cut with a knife. While in prison, Jesse was treated as a dangerous inmate and was kept in solitary confinement for forty-one years.

Another teen killer, fifteen-year-old Louis Hamlin, committed a crime that mirrors the mode of operation of many of today's serial killers. In 1981, he, along with a friend, abducted two twelve-year-old girls walking through the woods in Vermont. The pair raped, stabbed, and shot both of the girls. Only one of the victims died. Louis had a history of previous violent crimes, and he was also alleged to have sexually abused his own sister.

In 1995, fifteen-year-old Edward O'Brien Jr., a former altar boy from Massachusetts, was convicted of killing his best friend's mother, Janet Downing, by stabbing her nearly one hundred times. He is alleged to have spied on her undressing from across the street. Police were led to believe that the crime was sexually motivated. Investigators who pieced together the details of the crime said that Edward waited until Janet was alone and asleep on her couch, and then he attacked her with the knife. During the crime he undressed and re-dressed her corpse.

A serial killer who killed with a sexual connection was Illinois' John Wayne Gacy, also known as the "Killer Clown," who killed in the Chicago area during the 1970s. As an adult he entertained children in the neighborhood, dressed up as a clown. He called himself "Pogo the Clown." He murdered a total of thirty-three boys, twenty-seven of whom he had buried underneath his house in a crawl space.

Gacy was a middle child who attended Catholic schools growing up and was active in the Boy Scouts as an adult volunteer. His alcoholic father was abusive and described his son as a sissy. When Gacy was sixteen, doctors discovered a blood clot in his brain that was caused by a severe blow to the head a few years earlier. He suffered from frequent blackouts as a result of the crushing blow.

Gacy got married at the age of twenty-one, and in that same year had his first homosexual encounter. He was arrested and convicted of child molestation at the age of twenty-six and began his killing spree four years later.

William Bonin, known as the "Freeway Killer," murdered between twenty-one and thirty-six victims in California, during the late seventies and early eighties. He cruised around in his van, sometimes with an accomplice, and picked up young male prostitutes or hitchhikers. These young men were abducted, raped, and then were brutally strangled to death. Bonin's youngest victim was only twelve years old.

Born in Connecticut to an alcoholic and gambling father and a mother who constantly ran away, Bonin was raised for the most part by his grandparents. His grandfather was a convicted child molester. At the age of eight, Bonin started carrying out various crimes, like stealing license plates. As the years passed by, he ended up serving a sentence in a juvenile detention center and was raped there by older boys. He moved back in with his mother when he was released in his teens and soon after began molesting younger children.

At the age of twenty-three, Bonin was sent to prison for sexually assaulting a young boy. Almost in the same breath, he was released and sent back again for raping a fourteen-year-old boy. After he completed his sentence, he made a vow to his friends that it was the last time he would ever be behind bars. Bonin decided the only way to prevent returning to prison was to kill his future victims. Bonin showed no remorse when captured and told reporters that he simply couldn't stop killing. In 1996, he was executed by lethal injection.

A CLOSE AND PERSONAL METHOD OF KILLING

When a killer chooses a more personal and up-close method of murder, it signifies a different type of killer. Many of the killers in this category kill with a knife, rope, tire iron, or even their bare hands, as opposed to using a gun or setting a fire, which is a more distant and less intimate way to kill another person.

One particular crime involved four teenage girls in Indiana; it truly stunned me when I first came across it in the course of my research. The two ringleaders of the group—seventeen-year-old Lauri Tackett and sixteen-year-old Melinda Loveless—carried out most of the violence in this crime and definitely exhibited serial-killer tendencies. In 1992, these girls kidnapped, tortured, and killed a twelve-year-old girl who was an acquaintance of theirs, beating her with a tire iron and then setting her on fire. The victim was kept alive for hours in the trunk of their car as Melinda and Lauri drove around trying to decide how to finish her off. At one point, Lauri smelled the blood on the end of the tire iron and laughed.

Another teen murder in this category occurred in Alabama. Sixteen-year-old Mark Anthony Duke and nineteen-year-old Brandon Samra killed four people in a brutal fashion. Duke first shot and killed his father in the kitchen because he wouldn't allow him to use his truck. After his father was dead, he murdered his father's girlfriend and her two young children. These three people were killed in serial-killer fashion. He first shot the mother, but the gunshot wound didn't kill her. The two teens chased down the mother and her two children, who were able to lock themselves into a bathroom. They broke the door down, shot the mother in the forehead, and used a knife to cut the throats of the two small children.

This kind of crime is much different from that of a school shooter opening fire with a handgun, and is an up-close and personal murder, much more intimate. This is a sign of possible continuing future violence.

THE BOSTON STRANGLER

The most popular case in crime history in which the mode of killing hints at serial murder has to be Albert DeSalvo, also known as the "Boston Strangler." He spread fear throughout the city of Boston when his killing spree claimed the lives of thirteen women from 1962 to 1964. After he sexually assaulted each young lady, he strangled her with an article of her clothing and knotted the noose into a bow to leave his signature.

DeSalvo was born in 1931 and was the product of a nasty divorce. His alcoholic father was known for bringing home prostitutes and even engaged in sexual intercourse in front of his son. DeSalvo grew up in a poverty-stricken area and sold himself to homosexuals around the community. His first sexual experience occurred at the age of ten, which inflamed his unusual sexual appetite. This later drove him to commit murder.

In the late fifties—in two unrelated events—the army discharged him, and his wife left him. DeSalvo created a job where he took the measurements of young women and promised them possible modeling opportunities. He became known as the "Measuring Man." Involved in petty crimes during this time, DeSalvo was eventually charged and convicted in a breaking and entering case. Upon his release from prison in 1962, he believed it was time for him to seek revenge against women.

DeSalvo began his nineteen-month murder spree and became known as the "Boston Strangler." His victims were both young and old. Some were raped; others were purposefully posed in weird sexual positions. He even robbed a couple of them after he killed them. After DeSalvo murdered his last victim, he embarked on a rape spree, during which he sexually assaulted approximately three hundred women. He ended up in a maximum security prison, where he was stabbed to death by another inmate.

INSIDE THE MIND OF A TEEN KILLER

AMERICA'S MOST INFAMOUS SERIAL KILLER

Another famous serial killer who displayed typical serial-killer tendencies in his mode of murder was Theodore Robert "Ted" Bundy, who was responsible for the deaths of many young women in a multitude of states between 1974 and 1978. This charming killer was famous for using his good looks to lure young women on college campuses, in shopping malls, in apartment buildings, and once even in a grade school. His ideal victim was a pretty brunette who parted her hair down the middle and bore a striking resemblance to an ex-girlfriend. Bundy's former girlfriend had rejected him, and the breakup may have contributed to his violent tendencies against women.

Bundy's story is fascinating because of his handsome appearance and successful image. No one suspected that this intelligent, charismatic guy was a violent, cannibalistic killer who had sex with the corpses of his victims. Bundy had several ruses that worked to lure young women into his car. Many times he wore a fake cast on his arm to make his victims feel sorry for him. Their pity prompted them to help him with whatever it was he needed. Bundy beat most of his victims unconsciousness, raped them, sodomized them, bit them, and strangled them.

In his confession on death row, Bundy admitted to killing thirty women and decapitating at least a dozen of his victims with a hacksaw. He had kept the severed heads in his apartment for some time before disposing of them. He also confessed to visiting his victims' bodies over and over again, stating that he would lie with them for hours, apply makeup to their faces, and have sex with their decomposing bodies. Some speculate that Bundy could have killed more than one hundred people. What made this intelligent, handsome, University of Washington honors graduate transform into a cannibalistic serial killer?

Bundy was born in 1946 to a single mother. He never met his biological father, who was an air force veteran. Shortly after his birth, Bundy's mother moved them into her parents' home and falsely led her son to believe that his grandparents were his parents, and that she was his sister. An incident with his aunt while he was only three years old was a strong indication that perturbing violent and sexual thoughts were in the making. One day his aunt woke up from a nap, surrounded by knives. Toddler Bundy stood by the bed, smiling at her.

When he was a still a young boy, his mother married a military cook by the name of Johnnie Culpepper Bundy. Ted instantly became a stepbrother to four siblings. His new stepfather tried to bond with him, but Bundy never allowed it.

He considered his grandfather to be his role model. In a 1987 interview with Dorothy Lewis, Bundy said that his grandfather tortured animals. He beat the family dog and swung neighborhood cats by their tails. He also said that his grandfather, who was a deacon in his church, stashed a large collection of pornography in his greenhouse. Bundy and a cousin would sneak into the greenhouse for hours at a time, soaking their minds and eyes in the filth. Later, Bundy pointed to violent pornography as a major factor in his crimes.

Though he was a good student at school, involved with the Boy Scouts, and even served as the president of the Methodist Youth Fellowship, Bundy had a dark side that no one knew about. It would soon completely possess his soul and cost dozens of innocent young ladies their lives. While Bundy participated in healthy extracurricular activities to hide his evil facet, his notorious compulsions were becoming more apparent. He started to shoplift with a passion, a sign many experts attribute to a budding psychopath. While on death row, Bundy described his dark side and admitted that he had been fascinated by images of sex and violence from a young age. He was executed in "Old Sparky," Florida's electric chair, on January 24, 1989.

THE GAINESVILLE RIPPER

One of the most brutal and shocking killers of all time was serial killer Danny Rolling, or "the Gainesville Ripper," who was executed in 2006, convicted of committing many horrible crimes, including the murder and mutilation of a number of young women. He admitted to eight murders and three rapes and confessed to three more murders days before his execution. Inspired by the movie *Exorcist III*, which portrays an evil spirit with the name Gemini, Rolling created an alter ego for himself with the same name. His crimes mirrored those shown in the film.

Before Rolling killed his victims, he told them his step-by-step plan as to

One of the last prison photos of serial killer Danny "the Gainesville Ripper" Rolling, who sent me a few letters and a few drawings shortly before his execution. Rolling murdered young college coeds, and sometimes decapitated and staged their dead bodies.

how he would go about the murders. In one of his crimes, Rolling decapitated a young woman and placed her head on a shelf for the police to find when they arrived. He was also notorious for posing his victims postmortem in an attempt to shock whoever found the bodies.

Rolling had been mentally, physically, and emotionally abused by his father, who was a police officer and who had also abused Rolling's mother and his younger brother. Professionals testified at his murder trial that because of the tremendous amount of abuse Rolling endured during childhood, he functioned as an adult at the maturity level of a fifteen-year-old. He was locked up several times as a teen and a young adult for robberies he committed in Georgia. When he fled to Florida, he erupted into a serial killer and murdered college students in the town of Gainesville, Florida.

I corresponded with Rolling before his execution and found him to be an incredibly sad and depressed man. He was executed on October 26, 2006.

NECROPHILIA: HAVING SEX WITH DEAD VICTIMS

Obviously, some will claim that when you commit necrophilia, you must be mentally ill. In my opinion, whether mental illness is present or not, it is a true sign of serial-killing behavior. When teens take part in this type of crime, it usually indicates a serial killer in the making.

In 1979, seventeen-year-old Jay Kelly Pinkerton from Texas killed his neighbor, a mother of three, by stabbing her thirty times and slitting her throat. He then had sexual intercourse with her body. Jay was caught, convicted, and sentenced to death. He was also convicted of another sexual murder in

Texas, in which he raped and stabbed another woman. He died at the hands of the state by lethal injection in 1986.

Another teen murder in this category took place in Alabama. It shocked even seasoned detectives and investigators and involved two seventeen-year-olds. Kenneth Loggins and Trace Duncan picked up a hitchhiker, an adult female, and took her to a secluded area where they tortured and killed her. They threw bottles at her and kicked and beat her for thirty minutes until she was dead, even stepping on her neck. They then sexually molested her body and, when finished, threw her over a cliff.

What makes this case even more troubling, and speaks volumes about the offenders, is that they returned to the body and stabbed it approximately 180 times. They then removed parts of her body, including her fingers and thumbs. They allegedly took bites out of parts of her body. This is a perfect example of teenagers who are on a very fast track to becoming serial killers.

Many serial killers have included necrophilia in their crime sprees, including Edmund Kemper, who was known as the "Co-Ed Killer." He was a very large, intimidating man from California who murdered nine people. He stood just three inches shy of seven feet and weighed three hundred pounds. Kemper earned his nickname from six of his victims who were co-eds. He used various methods of murder, but dismembered and had sex with most of his victims.

Kemper's childhood was strange at best. His mother verbally abused him and locked him in their basement at night to protect his sisters. As a child he tortured and killed animals, including the family cat. He also cut the heads off his sisters' dolls and acted out bizarre sexual rituals with those dolls. Kemper was eventually locked up in a state hospital and was then released to his mother's care, which proved to be a fatal mistake. Kemper murdered his mother and had sex with her corpse.

Kemper said, "I have fantasies about mass murder . . . I make mad passionate love to their dead corpses. Taking life away from them . . . and then having possession of everything that used to be theirs. All that would be mine. Everything."[2]

Serial killers who practiced necrophilia include Jeffrey Dahmer, Richard Chase, Dennis Nilson, Jerry Brudos, Ted Bundy, and Gary Ridgeway (the Green River Killer). Dennis Nilson often kept dead bodies in his bed for sexual purposes for a week after he killed them.

PSYCHOPATHIC BEHAVIOR

The fourth element of a crime that displays serial murder tendencies is psychopathic behavior. This is a personality disorder or a psychological disorder that leads a person to commit crimes and display actions that may seem insane or mentally ill. This person is not mentally ill and can lead a normal life and blend in to society.

Some people with this disorder feel like killing for no other reason than to experience the act of killing. Matthew Rooy from Michigan fits into this category. In 2001, nineteen-year-old Matthew killed his girlfriend. He picked her up in the middle of the night and told her they were going to have some "fun." In his confession, investigators related that Matthew had been thinking about committing murder for a long time. Matthew told me that he had been sexually abused by a babysitter growing up and suffered from depression and suicidal thoughts that eventually transformed into distinctive imaginings of murder. He feels terrible for what he did; even today he still cannot figure out why he had such a strong urge to kill another human being.

Jeffrey Dahmer was a cannibal killer who got his start in Bath, Ohio, and eventually moved his crime spree to Wisconsin. One of the most infamous serial killers of our day because of the grotesque nature of his crimes, Dahmer was responsible for the deaths of seventeen males between 1978 and 1991. When he was only fourteen, he had fantasies about murdering men and having sex with their corpses. He was also fascinated with dead animals and rode around town with garbage bags to collect the remains of dead animals for his own private cemetery. He stripped the flesh off these animals, and one time he mounted a dog's head on a stick for fun.

Dahmer was eighteen years old when he committed his first murder. He picked up a hitchhiker in Bath, Ohio, and invited the man to his home to drink some beer and fool around in a sexual sense. After they had intercourse and the man got up to leave, Dahmer hit him in the head with a barbell, instantly killing him. He then decapitated the dead hitchhiker, cut off his body parts, placed them in garbage bags, and buried them in his backyard.

Dahmer embarked on his Milwaukee killing spree in 1991, at the age of thirty-one. He killed his victims, had sex with their corpses, and ate the body parts. He stashed some body parts in his house. When police officers searched his residence, they were horrified to find the heads of many of his victims in his refrigerator. Dahmer was convicted and sentenced to life in a Wisconsin prison, where another inmate killed him in a racially motivated attack.

A psychopath who started very young was Carroll Edward Cole, a serial killer who murdered sixteen victims in California, Nevada, and Texas. As I mentioned earlier, he made his first kill at the age of eight, when he drowned a classmate and pretended it was an accident. Cole's family life started to collapse when he was only six years old. In the early forties, his father had left the family when he was drafted to serve in World War II. Cole's mother frequently engaged in drunken sex with a number of soldiers and violently beat her son so that he would not tell his father what was happening. This occurred on many occasions, and the beatings unfortunately got worse.

The abuse Cole endured took a toll on him and fueled his future violent behavior. One time he blacked out and woke up under the house porch. He discovered he had strangled the family dog during his blackout. He also began to experience horrific daydreams about killing his mother, or any other female for that matter. Cole went on to kill sixteen people; he picked up most of his victims at bars. He confessed to his crimes after being captured and was executed by lethal injection in 1985.

It is amazing to me how depraved human beings can become, and how shocking their crimes against other human beings can be. The offenders mentioned in this chapter were born into families, as we all were, but something went terribly wrong as they grew up. Many of these serial killers were raised in very unstable families, which led them down the path to murder. I would strongly urge you to keep your eyes and ears open in your neighborhood, in your community, and even in your family, and do anything you can to help children who are being abused or who may be living in a severely dysfunctional home. You might be able to help prevent the formation of a serial killer.

FOR MORE INFORMATION ON TEEN MURDER
AND THE CASES COVERED IN THIS BOOK,
LOG ON TO WWW.PHILCHALMERS.COM.
DON'T MISS PHIL'S BOOK,
THE ENCYCLOPEDIA OF TEEN KILLERS.

ELEVEN

COLUMBINE, MUNICH-STYLE: TEEN KILLERS INTERNATIONALLY

> One day, I want everyone to know my name
> and I want to be famous.
>
> —ROBERT STEINHAEUSER,
> "the Erfurt Terminator,"
> German school shooter, as told to a classmate

If you are an American and were asked to name the most deadly high school shooting, you would probably think of the 1999 Columbine massacre that killed twelve students and a teacher and wounded twenty-four others. I'm sure many of you would also be reminded of the 2007 Virginia Tech tragedy that left thirty-two people dead. But did you know that the deadliest high school shooting happened in Germany?

Youth violence is more than just an American problem; it is an international epidemic. Murders carried out by the hands of young people regularly occur in many countries, even in those nations that have tight gun control laws or even ban guns completely. When teenagers are intent on killing, they will use whatever legal or illegal weapons they can get their hands on.

As you read the stories in this chapter, focus your attention on the type of weapon used in the crimes. Not all of them are guns. While some people advocate tougher gun control laws—including controversial celebrities like Rosie O'Donnell and Michael Moore—and strongly suggest that guns are the main reason teenagers are turning into killers, it is not necessarily the case.

The problem of teen killing runs much deeper than the dangers or accessibility of guns.

Comparing murder rates with other countries is a challenging task because many of the statistics vary to a large degree from one study to the next. Research conducted by United Nations committees, however, seems to be the most reliable. According to the *Seventh United Nations Survey of Crime Trends and Operations of Criminal Justice Systems*,[1] below are the top ten countries with the highest murder rates from 1998 to 2000:

1. Colombia
2. South Africa
3. Jamaica
4. Venezuela
5. Russia
6. Mexico
7. Estonia
8. Latvia
9. Lithuania
10. Belarus

Believe it or not, the United States was ranked at the number twenty-four spot in this study. As far as other notable countries are concerned, France was ranked at forty, Australia at forty-three, Canada at forty-five, Spain at forty-eight, Germany at forty-nine, and Japan at sixty. Let me share some stories of teen killers across the globe. There are some definite common similarities with American teen killers.

GERMANY

On April 26, 2002, nineteen-year-old Robert Steinhaeuser, also known as the "Erfurt Terminator," went on a blood-drenched rampage at Johann Gutenburg Gymnasium in Erfurt, Germany. Clothed in a ninja outfit and a ski mask and armed with a pistol, a pump-action shotgun, and ammunition, Robert shot and killed thirteen teachers, two students, and a police officer and injured ten other people. The killing frenzy was over in about twenty minutes when the Erfurt Terminator killed himself after being locked in a classroom by a heroic teacher.

(AP Photo / THUERINGER ALLGEMEINE)

Robert Steinhaeuser killed seventeen people, including himself, in the deadliest school shooting in recent world history. The shooting took place in Erfurt, Germany, in 2002.

Most of the victims were killed by shots to the head. Investigators suggested that his targets were intended to be only teachers or other authority figures. Robert chased one particular teacher, who had tried to escape, out to her car. When she tripped, he fired three shots to her head. The woman died instantly.

Robert lived in a comfortable, middle-class home with his grandparents and his mother. He was a big fan of guns and had a license to own and use them. In high school, Robert created a disturbing film. The plot detailed a main character who took revenge on a gang for killing his girlfriend. Each gang member was killed execution-style with a gunshot to the head. The story concluded with the suicide of the gunman. Sounds almost exactly like what Robert did, doesn't it? The sad truth is that while students and teachers knew about this violent work, nobody talked to Robert about it to see if there was more to it than just an active imagination.

Investigators revealed that most of Robert's entertainment choices were laden with violence. He was a fan of violent computer games like *Counter Strike*, a first-person shooter game, and the death metal music group Slipknot. Robert also regularly read violent comic books and watched horror movies. Police officers found numerous articles on his computer about the Columbine killings. Perhaps he found his inspiration in American teen killers Eric Harris and Dylan Klebold. The shooting occurred six days after the third anniversary of the Columbine attacks.

Before the murders, Robert had taken the German equivalent of the

American SAT test, which he had flunked. Using a forged doctor's note, he avoided retaking the test and was subsequently expelled from school. This punishment proved to be too much for him to handle and pushed him to want to commit suicide. Instead of just killing himself, he decided to go out in a blaze of glory—the American teen killer way, in his mind—and take innocent lives with him.

This German school shooting manifested all the trappings of an American school shooting. A mother of one of the students remarked, "We've been Americanized."

I think it's very ironic that the deadliest school shooting occurred just hours after the German parliament approved a new bill tightening the country's already strict gun control laws.

Another German teen killer, eighteen-year-old Sebastian Bosse, stormed into the school yard of his former high school in Emsdetten in 2006 and opened fire. He shot five people, but all miraculously survived. Police found Sebastian dead on the second floor of the school with pipe bombs strapped to his body. Known as a misfit who was obsessed with violence, Sebastian had previously talked about his desire to commit suicide. On his Web site he also made public his desire to seek revenge on everyone who had wronged him. He wrote, "This revenge will be carried out so brutally and without quarter that the blood will freeze in your veins."[2]

CANADA

Our neighbor to the north has experienced its share of some pretty heinous crimes committed by teenagers. While many of the cases are recent, teen violence in Canada did not erupt overnight.

On May 28, 1975, sixteen-year-old Michael Slobodian opened fire on his classmates at Brampton Centennial Secondary School in Brampton, Ontario, Canada. Michael killed a fellow classmate and an English teacher and wounded thirteen others. He then committed suicide in one of the school's bathrooms.

Another early school shooting happened on October 21, 1975, when eighteen-year-old Robert Poulin opened fire with a shotgun on his class at the St. Pius X High School in Ottawa, Ontario, Canada. He killed one person and wounded five others. Following the pattern of many killers, Robert ended his act of rage by turning the gun on himself. Robert, who has been written about in the book *Rape of a Normal Mind*, was not a first-time offender.[3] Before this shooting, he had raped and stabbed his seventeen-year-old girlfriend.

On August 16, 1991, fifteen-year-old Gavin Mandin of Alberta, Canada, used a .22-caliber rifle to shoot to death several members of his family, including his mother, Susan; his stepfather, Maurice; and two younger sisters, twelve-year-old Islay and ten-year-old Janelle. All four victims were shot at close range. After slaying his family, Gavin discarded the corpses in a brushy area behind their home. He said he committed the crime because he hated doing household chores, and that he despised his mother and stepfather because they bugged him. Gavin was quoted as saying that he was perfectly justified in his actions. Charged and convicted, he is currently serving a life sentence in prison.

Eighteen-year-old James Bridson began his brutal rampage in May 1993 by abducting thirteen-year-old Meaghan McConnell in Manitoba. He then shot the little girl's mother and brother dead and also injured a fifteen-year-old teenage girl named Shannon. Meaghan lived. The murderous acts mirrored a movie that had recently aired on television, *Murder in the Heartland*, which detailed the biography of famed spree killer Charles Starkweather. It featured actors Randy Quaid and Brian Dennehy and was nominated for multiple Emmy awards. Investigators drew a connection between James's crime and the movie.

In January 1994, a thirteen-year-old boy from Whitehead, Nova Scotia, rang the doorbell of his neighbor's home and shot the married couple who opened the front door. The man was killed instantly and his wife was paralyzed. Though the teen killer shot them at random, his actions were fueled by his anger toward his father for refusing to buy him chewing tobacco.

Three teenagers—ages thirteen, fourteen, and fifteen—from Montreal killed an Anglican priest, Frank Troope, and his wife, Jocelyn, in 1995. Both victims were seventy-five years old and were found bludgeoned to death with a baseball bat in their home. The killers were motivated by the thrill of the crime.

In Saskatchewan in 1996, fourteen-year-old Sandy Charles murdered a seven-year-old boy. Sandy said he was fascinated with the horror movie *Warlock* and its sequel, and watched the film ten times before he killed and mutilated the little boy. The fatal injuries found on the child victim replicated those of a murder victim in the movie.

Leroy Linn, eighteen, received a life sentence in Saskatchewan in May 1997 for killing Diane McLaren and Sandra Veason. During the trial, prosecutors asserted that Leroy not only bragged about the crime but told others that he was a "natural born killer." It is believed that this teen killer was mimicking the behavior of Woody Harrelson's character from the movie *Natural Born Killers*.

A recent case that stunned authorities involved a twelve-year-old girl by the name of Jasmine Richardson from Medicine Hat, Alberta. On April 23, 2006, Jasmine and her twenty-three-year-old boyfriend, Jeremy, killed Jasmine's father, her mother, and her eight-year-old brother. Because she was so young, Jasmine was only sentenced to ten years, the maximum penalty according to Canadian law. She became the youngest person ever charged with multiple killings in Canadian history.

On various Web sites, this young teen killer had included in her profile a description of herself as bisexual, Wiccan, nocturnal, insane, and a deep thinker. She listed her interests as "poetry, criminal psychology, blood, human anatomy, and kinky s—t." Both Jasmine and Jeremy were heavily involved in the gothic lifestyle and adorned their Web pages with corresponding dark themes, verbiage, and symbols.

UNITED KINGDOM

On June 23, 1973, thirteen-year-old Peter Dinsdale, from Hull, England, killed six-year-old Richard Ellerington by burning him to death in his own bed. Peter, nicknamed "the Holocaust Man," then went on to terrorize northern Britain for the next six years, killing twenty-five people during that time frame. Included among his victims were two babies, elderly women, and numerous children.

A pyromaniac and arsonist, he used fire in many of the crimes. In one fire he set in a retirement home, eleven people were killed. Peter was epileptic and slightly deformed. He had his name legally changed to Bruce Lee, in honor of his Kung Fu hero. At the time of the murders, he was living in a Salvation Army homeless shelter.

Peter came from a very unstable family. His mother was a prostitute. He made the following statement after his crime spree: "I've done well to become that famous, haven't I, considering my background?" Peter was sentenced to life in a prison for the criminally insane.

In January 1999, after watching the movie *Scream*, two thirteen-year-old boys from London stabbed a mutual friend eleven times in the head and left him to die. The victim, who survived but sustained permanent brain damage and partial paralysis, was found forty hours later. He was partially hidden in a garbage can liner in the woods. Lucky to be alive, the boy told investigators that he had heard his attackers discussing where best to stab someone, and immediately afterward felt one of the disturbed boys ramming a knife into his head.

FRANCE

In Paris in early 1995, a nineteen-year-old female and her twenty-two-year-old boyfriend stole a few guns from French police and hijacked a taxi. They put a gun to the taxi driver's head and went on a joy ride until the taxi driver drove into a police car on purpose. After the crash, the couple killed the taxi driver and two police officers while screaming lines from the movie *Natural Born Killers* at each other. They fled the scene and were chased by a third policeman on a motorcycle, whom they later shot and killed. A second shoot-out with police occurred, and the fired shots managed to hit the boyfriend, who was instantly killed. The female teen was charged and convicted of killing five people.

In March 2000, a sixteen-year-old Parisian teen stabbed his father and stepmother to death the day after the movie *Scream 3* was released in movie theaters. He wore the same mask as the one sported by the main character. French media reported that another teen was arrested following the release of the same movie. This young man was found near a suburban train, carrying a kitchen knife and dressed as the *Scream* killer.

BRAZIL

On March 7, 2000, a nine-year-old boy in San Paulo, Brazil, stabbed a neighborhood girl three days after he watched the horror film *Child's Play 2*. He used three serrated knives as his weapons of choice. The little girl miraculously survived because the attempted killer was "small and didn't have enough physical strength" to plunge the knife into her body hard enough, according to crime scene inspector Susana Machado. Ms. Machado reported, "I've never seen a child attack another with such violence."

JAPAN

A twelve-year-old boy from Nagaski, Japan, kidnapped, molested, and killed a four-year-old child in July 2003. That same month, a fourteen-year-old teen from Okinawa beat a fellow thirteen-year-old child to death.

On February 14, 2005, a seventeen-year-old in Osaka, Japan, stabbed a teacher to death and seriously wounded two others at his former elementary school. After he slashed his victims, he took a break and stood in the teacher's lounge, smoking a cigarette with the bloody knife still in his hand. His choice of weapon is commonly used in Japan for gutting fish.

Other recent teen offenders in Japan include:

- A previously well-behaved fifteen-year-old who stabbed a neighboring family of six, killing three, after he was accused of being a Peeping Tom.
- A seventeen-year-old boy who hijacked a bus in southwestern Japan, fatally stabbing a sixty-year-old woman with a sixteen-inch knife and injuring five others,
- A seventeen-year-old student who stabbed to death a sixty-five-year-old woman because he "wanted to experience killing someone."

According to Pulitzer-nominated author Lt. Col. Dave Grossman, the number of murders by juveniles in Japan doubled from 1998 to 1999. Japan's former chief cabinet secretary Kanezo Muraoka told Reuters in a 1998 interview, "I think the younger generation lacks the basic ethical sense of the importance of life and the difference between good and bad."[4] He stated his opinion after a fourteen-year-old boy chopped off and mutilated the head of an eleven-year-old child in 1998. This case prompted Japanese lawmakers to lower the age of criminal responsibility and accountability from sixteen to fourteen.

Also, it seems that the weapon of choice for many Japanese teen killers is the so-called butterfly knife, which is said to have become popular after a weekly television series portrayed teen celebrity Takuya Kimura using the knife.

SOUTH AMERICA

On September 28, 2004, a fifteen-year-old high school student in southern Argentina opened fire in a classroom. He killed four classmates and wounded five others in the country's worst school rampage in history. The young man began the brutal attacks in silence, simply shooting with a 9mm handgun into a classroom as students cowered underneath their desks. The killer was arrested in the school yard and is facing a lengthy prison sentence.

RUSSIA

Dragoslav Petkovic, a seventeen-year-old who lived in the small impoverished town of Vlasenica, shot two teachers, killing one of them, on April 29, 2002. Dragoslav then committed suicide. Witnesses said the teen killer approached one of the teachers in the school yard and asked him for another chance to improve his grade. He ended up killing the teacher with a handgun. He then rushed into the school building and burst into a classroom where his fifty-year-old math instructor was teaching. Though he shot her in the neck, she survived the shooting. Seconds later, the eleventh grader put the gun to his head and pulled the trigger in front of thirty terrified students.

In the Siberian town of Talmenka, a thirteen-year-old schoolboy was outraged after his parents beat him for getting bad grades at school. He felt he had to retaliate. In the early morning hours the following day, the teen killer took his father's double-barreled shotgun, crept into his parents' bedroom, and shot and killed them while they slept in bed. He originally intended to throw their bodies into a river, but he couldn't start the car he would have needed to transport the corpses. Instead, the thirteen-year-old placed the bodies in a closet, where his sister discovered them the next day. The boy was quoted as saying, "My father never used to punish me for school marks . . . this time he turned into a brute."[5]

TURKEY

Sixteen-year-old Ogun Samast shot and killed an Armenian journalist in January 2007 because he didn't agree with the journalist's views on the genocide of Armenians by Turks in the early twentieth century. Ogun's father, who was riding a bus home from Istanbul that day, noticed his son's picture on television as someone wanted for murder. He had no choice but to turn his boy over to authorities. When he was arrested, Ogun confessed to the crime. The teen is awaiting trial at the time of this writing.

NEW ZEALAND

In Auckland, New Zealand, a fifteen-year-old boy was arrested for the murder of a seventy-seven-year-old woman. The woman had been stabbed numerous times, and some of the wounds had pierced her vital organs. The police considered the violent and bloody scene among the worst they had seen.

NAMIBIA

Two childhood friends raped and murdered a female friend of theirs in Namibia on December 26, 1998. Intoxicated, the boys committed what has been referenced as one of the most savage crimes in recent Namibian history. The boys, ages fifteen and sixteen, raped their victim, slit her throat with a broken bottle, stabbed her in the chest with the same bottle, and mutilated her breast. They completed the massacre by dropping a forty-pound rock on her head. Both boys came from unstable, broken homes. When describing their motive, the older of the two teens explained, "That [the murder] was actually not my intention. And I was under the influence of liquor."[6]

DENMARK

In November 2003, a fourteen-year-old Danish girl stabbed to death her eighteen-year-old brother and their father. The teen girl had psychological problems and loved to watch horror movies. Her brother was sleeping in his bedroom when the teen attacked him, stabbing him with a bread knife. When their father heard the commotion in his son's bedroom, he threw open the door and found his daughter stabbing her brother to death. Wearing coveralls and a Halloween mask, the young lady then turned on her father and stabbed him repeatedly in the arms and head.

She took off immediately in the family car, and police apprehended her after a brief car chase. It was reported that the girl was very interested in the occult and, according to her friends, had watched *Halloween* almost daily. Because of her age, she was not prosecuted but was sent instead to a mental hospital.

AUSTRALIA

On June 18, 2006, two seventeen-year-old girls in Sydney, Australia, murdered a fifteen-year-old-girl by strangling her to death. The three girls were having a sleepover, when one girl began to strangle the victim with a wire from an audio speaker. The other girl held a chemical-soaked cloth over the victim's face at the same time. They disposed of her corpse in a shallow grave under a house. The female teen killers told police that they knew it was wrong to kill, but it "felt right."[7] They expressed no remorse for the murders. Prosecutors recounted, "[They] planned the murder with calmness, consideration, emotional detachment and the desire to have the experience of killing someone."[8]

It's obvious that other countries besides the United States have to deal with the overwhelming issue of teen murder and violence. Unfortunately, many international murders are influenced by our violent, death-infused American media culture. We know the horrifying effect entertainment has on our own teenagers. The more we sell our poisonous culture to other countries, the more violence we will be spreading. Youth violence is a global concern that needs to be addressed on an international level—before it's too late.

For more information on teen murder
and the cases covered in this book,
log on to www.PhilChalmers.com.
Don't miss Phil's book,
The Encyclopedia of Teen Killers.

TWELVE

RAISING A KILLER
IN TEN EASY STEPS

It's easy now to see the signs: how a video-game joystick turned
[Eric] Harris into a better marksman . . . How [Dylan] Klebold's
violent essays for English class were like skywriting his intent. If
only the parents had looked in the middle drawer of Harris'
desk, they would have found the four windup clocks that he
later used as timing devices. Check the duffel bag in the closet;
the pipe bombs are inside . . . The problem is that until April 20,
nobody was looking. And Harris and Klebold knew it.

—NANCY GIBBS AND TIMOTHY ROCHE,
"The Columbine Tapes," *Time*, December 12, 1999

American psychologist and television personality Dr. Phil had this to say
about the problematic mind-set of today's parents: "They're [parents] intimi-
dated. Life is moving so fast and there's so much competition for influencing
their children that they're a little taken aback by it. Parents aren't the only
influence in their kids' lives, so they need to be the best, the loudest, the clear-
est and the closest."[1]

It would be easy to tell you what *not* to do to avoid raising a violent child
or would-be criminal or murderer. Instead I decided to reverse the approach
and advise on what you *should* do if you want your son or daughter to grow
up to be a teen killer. I understand there is no humor in homicide, but my
aim is for you to see reality through absurdity and to realize that making the
right (or wrong) choices in parenthood do make a difference. If you are not

a parent, this chapter will help guide you in noticing suspicious behavioral patterns in potentially violent teens. We are all responsible to create a better future, and part of that means paying attention to and investing in the younger generation. Our future and our world are at stake.

In my opinion, the following ten steps are the best way to point your children in the direction of drug and alcohol abuse, prostitution, murder, robbery, burglary, and assaults—you know, the basic life of crime. Whatever you do, do not take this list lightly. These are the most common mistakes parents and guardians make with their children. Do you want to spend the rest of your life communicating with your own flesh and blood through snail mail and by visits to state facilities? If you do, follow the advice in this chapter.

So—how do you raise a killer in ten easy steps?

STEP ONE:
PROVIDE AN UNSTABLE ENVIRONMENT

Here are some ideas. Create a broken home from a nasty and unnecessary divorce. You might consider bringing into your home boyfriends or girlfriends who are hostile or simply do not like your kids. You may even want to remarry— a couple of times—and subject your kids to numerous different "moms" and "dads" and a menagerie of stepsiblings.

As a parent, you can up the ante and sexually, physically, emotionally, mentally, or verbally abuse your child. Or surround him with other family members or friends who could do it for you. Another way to maintain a shaky home life is to have your child witness domestic violence. Be sure to pick a spouse or a boyfriend who likes to push you around or beat you up.

Instability can also be created outside of the family and home. Allowing your children to hang around peers who are bad influences is a guaranteed means for them to slide down the rocky slope of crime. Be sure to turn a blind eye and let your kids hang out with whoever, whenever, wherever. The most important thing is not to be an active positive influence in where they go or whom they choose to call their friends.

Bullying is a leading cause of teen murder and particularly school shootings, so the best way to ensure your child is negatively affected by its influence is to allow bullies to flourish at local schools, at extracurricular events, and even on school buses. Maintain a lax policy when it comes to bullying, and engage the mind-set that "all kids are bullied; it's just a gateway to growing up." If your child is a bully, pat him on the back and congratulate him. If your child is being bullied, just tell him or her to stop whining and buck up.

STEP TWO:
PROVIDE THEM WITH FREEDOM TO ABUSE DRUGS AND ALCOHOL

Situate your kids in an environment where they are exposed to dangerous substances like drugs and alcohol. These substances, along with mind-altering medication, will almost assure your child will—somehow, someday, in some way—get involved in violent crime, not to mention be bound by the harrowing monster of addiction. Many of the teen killers I meet say they would not have committed the unspeakable violence they carried out if it hadn't been for the conscience-searing, mind-numbing chemicals they ingested. These are the same kinds of drugs that are on the streets today and are available to every child, including your own. They are designed to make a person think less clearly and act without reason, and they can cause great medical and physical harm. Illicit drugs also have a knack for magnifying the current negative problems your teens may be experiencing at school or at home.

If you want your kids to start abusing drugs, you must continue with the first step in providing an unstable habitat and, especially, permitting them to befriend a peer who uses narcotics or alcohol. Forget about encouraging them to participate in extracurricular activities like sports or music. Give them the gift of freedom to smoke up, shoot up, or get wasted. This way they will have no accountability in their lives.

Another great idea is to pump your kids full of dangerous prescription medication in the hopes that these pills can substitute for good parenting. Why delve deeper into their psyche or invest more time and energy in being a better mom or dad when you can just give them more pills? Forget about spending quality time with or enjoying the company of your children—medicate them.

Finally, lead by example. Be sure your kids see you abuse drugs and alcohol. They will feel encouraged to follow in your footsteps. Remember, negative or even absent role modeling is the safest way for your kids to learn and live out these bad behaviors.

STEP THREE:
PROVIDE YOUR KIDS REGULAR ACCESS TO VIOLENT ENTERTAINMENT

Introducing your kids to violence like rape, sodomy, murder, pornography, graphic sex, and drug use is most effective if they can see it with their own eyes on a television or movie screen, listen to it on their iPods, or even manipulate video game characters to pretend to act out violence. Although children may accidentally stumble across these negative influencers at a young age, if they have zero accountability and no boundaries in the home, they will acquaint themselves with violence at a much quicker rate.

Young people have a way of visualizing violent entertainment as reality because their brains are not yet fully developed. Even intelligent kids have been known to take entertainment much more seriously than it was created to be. Eric Harris, one of the sick masterminds behind the Columbine massacre, is one such example. When he wrote about his killing spree in his journal, Eric combined his favorite video games with real events, believing the two were connected with reality. "It'll be like the L.A. riots, the Oklahoma bombing, WWII, Vietnam, *Duke* [violent video game], and *Doom* [violent video game] all mixed together . . . I want to leave a lasting impression."

Perhaps you don't think of television as a negative influence. Think again. How many school shootings have you heard of that were committed by kids in the Amish community, for example, or any other group of people who shuns this form of entertainment? Even further, how many teenagers with near-zero access to violent entertainment in general have committed murder? There are none on record. So just tell your kids they can watch whatever they want on TV. You may consider upgrading your cable or satellite package to include adult channels to maximize the amount of violence and obscenity available in the home.

If your child attends a movie theater, don't monitor what movies they see. Who cares if they tell you they are going to see *Shrek* when they can sneak into the theater showing *The Texas Chainsaw Massacre*? Kids are just naturally rebellious, right? They are going to do whatever they want anyway. Refrain from policing their Internet activity at the home or the DVDs they watch in their room with their friends or the video games they stockpile in the basement. The more violence, bloodshed, murder, rape, and obscenity your kids consume, the better chance they have at acting out the violence in real life, possibly even on you or your family.

Here's another nifty suggestion: as you remain clueless about the violent entertainment purchases your children make, why not make the purchases yourself? Gore porn is great as a birthday gift, as a stocking stuffer for Christmas, or even as a basket filler for Easter.

STEP FOUR:
DO NOT PROVIDE SPIRITUAL GUIDANCE AND DISCIPLINE FOR YOUR CHILDREN

There was a day when America was a God-fearing nation, and kids in school celebrated Christian holidays. They didn't have "winter break"; they had "Christmas break." They didn't have "spring break"; they had "Easter break." They were allowed to publicly pray in school and practice their religious beliefs. Our country was founded on God and inspired by moral principles, but things have sure changed since then.

If you want your kids to spend the rest of their lives behind bars, you must not teach them any spiritual disciplines. As a matter of fact, they must not be involved in anything spiritual, so their minds can be wide open to other beliefs that radiate hate, violence, murder, and perversion.

I like to encourage you, once again, to begin this habit by laying the groundwork for a spiritually devoid home. Skip church on Sunday, and watch television with your family instead. Better yet, you should go to work and leave your family at home to entertain themselves. If you are feeling guilty, you may consider sending your kids to church by themselves. This will create in them a sense of anger and resentment toward church, God, and, of course, you.

Be sure to interject your feeling and opinions about controversial subjects concerning religion. Support organizations like the ACLU and others who oppose religious principles and promote anti-God and antimoral philosophies. Write to your local and state politicians about abolishing the freedom to publicly pray in schools and, if you are feeling a bit ambitious, advocate the removal of the word *God* from public speech.

Discipline? Who needs discipline? Give your children the license to run free. Ensure they have no boundaries and definitely no consequences for any unscrupulous conduct. If you are effective, your children will start to dominate your household. Provide a lack of discipline from the time they are born so that when they are teenagers, it will be nearly impossible to control them. Eventually, they will not have any respect for you or other figures of authority.

Last, don't be alarmed if your kids start to experiment with dark religions or sects, like satanic cults, gangs, violent music fan clubs, or various hate groups. Kids without proper and loving spiritual guidance or discipline are easy prey for these various groups whose only desire is to manipulate and steal their minds, bodies, money, and souls. If you ignore your children for the most part, there is a really good chance they will meet someone who appears to love them more than you. This person can lead them to live a life of hate, depression, anger, and fear. Offer them plenty of privacy and freedom to establish deep and meaningful relationships with cult or gang members. The deeper they sink into these groups, the more difficult it will be to throw them a lifeline down the road and save them from inevitable destruction.

STEP FIVE: DON'T WORRY ABOUT YOUR KIDS' ANGER, DEPRESSION, OR MENTAL ILLNESS. THEY WILL OUTGROW IT

If you feel your child might have anger problems or suffer from depression or some type of mental illness, the best thing to do is nothing. Close your eyes and pretend that they are just being normal teenagers who will outgrow this troubling phase. Offering medical and psychiatric treatment or counseling will only prevent these problems from worsening. It may also stop them from experiencing homicidal fantasies. If you persist in ignoring their problems, it won't be long before they are pushed over the edge. They will feel like there are no other options left to fix their internal turmoil except to kill. Many teen killers I have talked to share this sentiment.

Another suggestion is to have a doctor or psychologist pump them full of mind-altering prescriptive drugs, especially those with warning signs or black boxes about possible side effects like depression, suicide, and homicide. Don't forget that drugs are a great alternative to good parenting.

STEP SIX:
IGNORE THE WARNING SIGNS
OF A VIOLENT TEEN

All sarcasm aside, let me first address common warning signs to observe in a possibly violent or murderous teen. Keep in mind that identifying these red flags can be tricky and sometimes even misleading. Some teens may exhibit a few of these signs and will never kill; others may have no outward hints of violence but will end up gunning down innocent people. While warning signs can manifest themselves in many ways, below are general indicators of a troubled teen.

- Making a statement or direct threat about harming or killing others
- Being fascinated with weapons
- Owning guns, knives, or other weapons
- Having one or all of the homicidal triad
- Coming from a violent family
- Having a history of mental illness
- Having verbal thoughts and conversations about death, murder, suicide, violence, and other dark concepts
- Spending excessive time watching or listening to violent entertainment
- Keeping a journal, a Web page, or other art forms filled with violent writings
- Being bullied and mistreated by others, especially at school
- Running away on numerous occasions
- Carrying out petty crimes, including vandalism and robbery
- Suffering from anger problems or depression
- Preferring to be isolated from family members and friends and avoiding social activities

- Not participating in any structured activity like sports, volunteer work, or youth group

Drawing of a person shooting a soccer player by Pearl, Mississippi, school shooter Luke Woodham. This is what we call a warning sign.

School writings of Pearl, Mississippi, school shooter Luke Woodham, with the lines "find death in chaos" and "one nation under my gun."

Now that we have some of point of reference as to what to look out for, if you want to raise a teen killer, *ignore these signs!* If you are a teacher and notice that little Johnny draws violent and bloody cartoons of people getting killed, just shrug your shoulders and move on to little Tina's picture of rainbows and butterflies. After all, violent drawings and death-filled art projects are supposed to be creative outlets for children, nothing more. If you are a fellow student and hear someone talk about killing others at school, shut your mouth and keep walking to gym class.

The principle of brushing off any abnormal changes, mood shifts, or violent behavior also applies to the home. Don't all teens, as they enter the growing years, change their hair color, style of dress, and opinions a hundred times a day? Don't all emotionally healthy kids dress in black and listen to Insane Clown Posse twenty-four hours a day? And what about that verbal threat your son just screamed? All kids say they want to kill their parents, right? After all, *your* child would never intentionally act on it. Your child is different—Johnny is a good boy!

As you magically wish away any alarming behavior your child is exhibiting, definitely do not talk to anyone about it. Friends, clergy, police, psychologists—what can they do? Nothing really. Nobody needs to know what goes on within the four walls of your home. It's private and it's your business. Shhhhh—don't talk or even think about your child's secret stash of knives and guns. Teen killers don't come from towns like yours. Gangbangers and homicidal maniacs only come from the big scary cities like Los Angeles or New York. They certainly don't come from quiet, rural, or even upscale towns like Jonesboro, Arkansas; Paducah, Kentucky; Littleton, Colorado; or Pearl, Mississippi.

STEP SEVEN:
DON'T SPEND TIME WITH YOUR CHILDREN

Remember the old days when families went on vacation together, ate dinner together, and went to church together? I'm pretty sure some of you are rolling your eyes reading this. Let's get real, right? Those days are long gone!

Kids do not want to spend quality time with their parents—they would rather have freedom, space, and time alone. So keep working and spending long hours at the office. Keep skipping dinner. Keep forgetting about your daughter's basketball games. Blow off your son's soccer games another year. When weekends come, even if you are physically home it is definitely much easier to throw a wad of bills at your kids' feet and tell them to entertain themselves. Besides, don't you need some peace and quiet? Kids are just annoying energy-zappers anyway. You need to take a nap, not spend quality time with them. Remember that the best—and cheapest—babysitter is the television. Actually, when I think about it, TV is the best parent or guardian replacement!

Finally, if you happen to go on vacation without your kids, consider letting them stay unsupervised at home or at a friend's house with parents whom you've never met. These are some great paths to provide a way for your kids to bond with others—and experiment with drugs or alcohol. They really need the opportunity to do things you would rather pretend they don't do.

STEP EIGHT:
ALLOW YOUR KIDS FULL ACCESS
TO YOUR WEAPONS, AND MAKE NO EFFORT
TO LOCK THEM UP

This is directed to you, Mr. or Mrs. Gun Owner. If you want your kids to kill, they need to secure weapons, right? Well, if you've got a gun at home, this is pretty easy stuff. Fall into the mental trap that your kids already know about guns and especially how dangerous they are. I'm sure adolescents have a deep respect for these weapons, and their curiosity will never get the best of them. After all, your kids grew up with guns in the house. Your son used to go hunting with you all the time. I'm sure that in all likelihood, they'll just ignore the gun you have propped up against the wall in your closet, hidden in your sock drawer, or just placed under your bed.

In fact, if you want to do this right, I have the best idea for storing your weapons. Purchase a pretty gun cabinet, you know, the kind with the cool carvings in the wood of jumping deer and flying mallards. Place all of your dangerous killing tools behind the most secure material known to man—a thin sheet of glass. Don't forget to keep that bottom drawer unlocked; you know how much of a hassle it is to look for a key when you want to get your ammunition out of your cabinet. By the way, keeping a gun fully loaded is another great idea. In case you decide to unload your weapon, be sure your children know where you store the ammunition so they don't have to spend their allowance on things like shotgun shells and hollow-point bullets.

Best of all, do what Kip Kinkel's parents did: reward your kids by buying them their own weapons. I'm sure you trust your teenage son or daughter, so just go for it! Go on, be a considerate and cool parent and buy them their own weapons. They make great graduation gifts!

STEP NINE:
CONTINUE TO LIVE IN A DANGEROUS NEIGHBORHOOD SO YOUR KIDS WILL FALL INTO A LIFESTYLE OF CRIME

I know many kids who have grown up in impoverished communities laden with violence, drugs, and gangs and have somehow found their way to end up as productive, law-abiding citizens. Unfortunately, statistically speaking, the chances are pretty slim. Most experts conclude that a child raised in such a brutal environment will likely take up that same lifestyle. The prison population proves this point. I speak to many men and women who grew up in horrific neighborhoods. They have told me that though they knew their parents loved them, they were basically left with few options for a bright future. The one choice that was pretty much guaranteed, however, was a life of crime.

If you live in a crime-infested, gang-ridden neighborhood, stay there. Just say your prayers and hope for the best. Believe what others say, and accept that this is the card you were dealt, and all you can do is learn how to survive. I know if you really wanted to, you could somehow find a way to escape the neighborhood, but it's probably too hard to even try. Besides, you grew up there, and you ended up somewhat okay. Who knows? Maybe your children will grow up and move into a safer neighborhood. Certainly, their future is not your responsibility. You are just there to make sure they have a place to sleep and some kind of food to eat.

STEP TEN:
NEVER TELL YOUR KIDS YOU LOVE THEM.

Showing affection toward your kids is so antiquated, isn't it? I mean, it's not like any of our families look or act like the Cleavers or the Brady Bunch. If you are a father, well, we all know that men who give hugs or offer words of encouragement are sissies. Under no circumstances should you hug, kiss, or tell your children how much you love them or how proud of them you are.

Do not model the true definition of unconditional love in the home. Your kids need to grow up with a distorted and unhealthy perspective of love and family. Forget about positive reinforcement. Pay attention only to the bad stuff they do, and discipline them in the worst sort of way for their mistakes. Don't worry, they will quickly get the point that they will never be able to please you, and so they might as well stop trying. Threaten them, hit them, beat them, scream at them, embarrass them, and degrade them. But whatever you do, never, never tell them you love them!

I may seem acerbic to some degree, but I feel so passionate about how we need to raise our kids. My message is one of love and hope, and the steps in this chapter are not to be taken literally. But they should rattle some cages and wake you up to the reality of how some of our kids—who will develop violent tendencies—are being raised.

I think that we, as parents, teachers, and community leaders, need to do our part in raising healthy, loved, and balanced children who live in safe surroundings with people who truly care for them and their futures. Every decision you make, particularly as a parent, does affect the lives of your children. It matters how you treat them. It makes a difference how you conduct your personal affairs.

As it concerns parenting, I think it's very important to wisely pick our battles and let the "small stuff" really stay the small stuff. On a personal note, I do have the tendency to be a bit of a perfectionist, and I realize that can really stress kids out. I constantly have to remind myself to focus on the critical issues and let the minor ones go.

I hope and pray that the information in this chapter has been helpful to you. Please work with me to do our best to eliminate the causes of teen murder. As members of society, we are all responsible for keeping our world as safe as possible. This starts first and foremost in the home. We must provide joy-filled, healthy, safe, and loving environments for our children that catapult them into successful lives as they grow older. If we take this matter seriously, a lot of good can be accomplished.

For help in parenting and other related issues, please refer to the resource section at the end of this book, titled "Phil Chalmers Recommends."

NOTE FROM THE AUTHOR:

If you read this chapter without paying attention to the first few paragraphs, please note that the sarcastic overtones were made on purpose. Refer to the beginning of the chapter for a detailed explanation.

CONCLUSION

KEEPING YOUR FAMILY, YOUR COMMUNITY, AND YOURSELF SAFE

Here are some practices that you can put into place to assure the safety of you and your family. Implement these guidelines and teach them to your children to decrease your chances and theirs of becoming another victim statistic of violent crime.

GENERAL TIPS

- When you are out and about, whether shopping, going for a jog, or running errands, be highly conscious of your surroundings. Never take shortcuts that would put you in isolated areas. Stay in populated areas.
- As you know, I'm a big believer in carrying protection of some kind. For a teenager, this could mean carrying a cell phone and possibly a can of high-powered pepper spray. For adults, many states now allow you to carry a concealed weapon, which I highly recommend. Acquiring a concealed carry permit is easy and worth the time and financial expense. If you choose this route of protection, spend plenty of time shooting your weapon at a gun range, and become highly knowledgeable of the ins and outs of guns. There is a lot to learn about handguns and the dangers of carrying a lethal weapon. You must also keep in mind that the weapons you

own could be used against you if you are unfamiliar with them and are not trained to use them properly and safely.

ESPECIALLY FOR YOUNG PEOPLE

- The first thing I tell young people is to never get into a stranger's car and never approach a random vehicle, no matter how the driver might be luring you. Keep at a safe distance in the event that you have to run away and get help. If someone is trying to kidnap you, never comply and willfully enter his vehicle. Do whatever you can to run away and fight, and do not initially comply with his demands. Even if he tells you he will not hurt you, chances are you will be hurt, possibly raped and tortured, and most likely killed.

- Never hitchhike or become involved in prostitution. Hitchhikers and prostitutes are common targets for serial killers and sexual predators, and they are the easiest type of murder victims.

- For teens especially, never go somewhere without telling your parents where you are. Do not sneak out of the house at odd hours of the night. This is very dangerous behavior, and many teens are no longer alive today because they decided to sneak out of their homes and party with their friends.

- Do not use the Internet as a channel for meeting new people. Today's predators are no longer lurking only at malls or at playgrounds. Many of them are using the Internet to stalk and eventually assault, rape, and even kill their prey. Web sites like MySpace, Facebook, and other such chat rooms should be used primarily to continue the friendships and relationships you already have. If you meet strangers using these means, you are putting yourself in harm's way. Refrain from advertising personal information about yourself, such as your address, phone number, or even the school you attend. Putting such things out in the public domain makes it much easier for a predator to track you down.

- Choose your friends wisely. I would suggest being very careful about who you hang out with. Befriending even casual acquaintances who seek after trouble and violence could land you in prison for life. If you are at the scene of a crime that your friends committed, you could go to jail for just being there! Always report illegal activity to the authorities. And to you female readers, stay away from the so-called "bad boys." Trust me, they are nothing but trouble.

In the Home

- Never allow strangers to enter your house, no matter who they are. If it's a postal worker, for instance, he can always leave whatever he is dropping off by the front door. On the same note, never open your door to speak to a stranger.
- Consider getting a watchdog like a German Shepherd or a Rottweiler who can be trained to protect you and your family against predators.
- Lock up guns or other deadly weapons in your home so children do not have access to them.

For Parents and Guardians

- Do your best to provide a stable environment for your family. Stay married when you can, and keep violence and abuse away from your children. Build a loving and protective hedge around your children, and shield them from negative influences—like pornography, cults, gangs, and bad friends who will drag your children down and toward destructive behaviors and activities.
- Keep your kids involved in positive activities like church functions, sports, and music lessons.
- Use your power and authority to keep your children away from violent entertainment. Monitor what they are watching, reading, and listening to. Do not give them the freedom to purchase entertainment without your approval first. Pay attention to what is entertaining them! This must start at a young age, while they are in the early years of elementary school. If you keep violent entertainment

away from them when they are young, chances are in your favor that they will not fall prey to this garbage as they get older.

- Teach your kids self-defense and other safety techniques, like how to be wary of suspicious or possibly violent adults and sexual predators.

- Most important, listen to your children and spend time with them. Most school shooters told someone what they were about to do but the ones who received the disturbing information made the tragic mistake of not taking it seriously. Andrew Williams, the fifteen-year-old shooter from Santana High School, threatened for days to bring a gun to school. Michael Carneal from Paducah, Kentucky, warned people not to come to school the day of his shooting. Kids need your time and not just things, so spend as much quality time as you can with them.

- Reach out to children who have absent or unhealthy families. Sometimes extending a listening ear, lending wisdom, and even welcoming a child into your home or family can make a huge difference in a child's life. And it really doesn't take that much effort. When you feel children you know are at some sort of risk, or possibly being abused or molested in their homes, call the authorities right away.

KEEPING YOUR SCHOOL AND COMMUNITY SAFE

The first thing we need to do to keep our schools and communities safe is to pull the heads of all school and community leaders out of the sand! Many of them are too naive to imagine that a violent crime or school shooting could happen in their neighborhood. I can't tell you how wrong that kind of thinking is. Pearl, Mississippi; Littleton, Colorado; Paducah, Kentucky; and Springfield, Oregon, are beautiful, comfortable, safe, and virtually all-American towns. They are also suburbs that were ravaged by crazed killers living right under their noses. Please don't make this mistake in your school and in your community. Take the approach that violence of any caliber *can* happen in your town and in your school!

The most commonsense step you can take is to learn the causes of teen murder I talked about in this book and become educated in what you can do to prevent these causal factors from occurring. Take responsibility as a citizen and report child abuse, turn in kids who are abusing drugs, and don't allow kids to be bullied and picked on at your school. Help keep violent entertainment out of your community, and notify the local authorities about adults who are selling this perversion to children in your town. Do what you can to educate other parents in your community who are blind to these causal factors.

Violence expert Lt. Col. Grossman called his strategy to keep schools safe "The Five Ds." His strategy includes the following wise recommendations:

- *Denial.* Stop living in denial. Violence exists, and even the most innocent-looking kid can do something dangerous. All of us, including school officials, must understand this.
- *Deter.* Deter school killers by not having a soft target. The best defense against violent criminals is to post armed police officers or school resource officers at every school. Teen mass murderers don't want to attack a school where they will get resistance.
- *Detect.* Be alert and catch killers before they strike. Be aware of and report suspicious behavior, like threats and bragging about violence. Grossman compared school killers to terrorists and pointed out the precautions we are taking to protect our country from these enemies. Take the same precautions at your schools and community centers.
- *Delay.* Learn how to delay a school shooter. Having secured classrooms with locked doors and protective wire mesh on the windows is a good example. At the Red Lake high school shooting in Minnesota, Jeff Weise broke into an unsecured room by busting the unsecured window and opening the door that a teacher was trying to hold shut. He killed several students and a teacher in a matter of minutes before the police arrived.

    At Columbine, school officials had no plan to deter potential violent offenders because no one imagined a crime of any caliber could take place in that upscale town. The teacher in the library did the best she could do with no safety plan and witnessed the execution of several of her students in the unsecured library. Columbine and Red Lake paid a huge price for not being prepared and not having a well-thought-out plan; the cost was nearly two dozen innocent victims. All schools have a fire drill, but few talk about a school-violence plan. What do you do when a shooting occurs? If your school has no plan or you have not practiced that plan, your head is now buried in sinking sand. All doors should be secured, and monitors should control who enters the school.

- *Defeat.* Today's police are being trained to apprehend or kill a school shooter. They will enter a school quickly and will use force if necessary. I'm sure we will never see law enforcement delay before entering a school as they did in Littleton.

Think about this. In America, we are scared to death of terrorists, and we are doing whatever we can to prevent another terrorist attack. These international criminals killed three thousand people on 9/11, but since that fateful day, teenagers have killed more than twelve thousand Americans, mostly other teenagers. The killers in our nation, including our youth, are much more dangerous and deadly than foreign terrorists. We need to start protecting ourselves against ourselves.

I'm not naive enough to think that a book can stop teen violence or that teen murder will one day just stop happening. But I do believe that we, as a society, can make a world of difference, and that together we can reach many kids before they reach this violent level—the willingness to end a human life. It's time the government and our leaders begin to make the decision to help kids who need our help. And we must stand together with and assist parents who are out of options with their violent teens. Let's start spending our dollars *now* and get these troubled kids the help they need, or we will, instead, be spending our money to apprehend and incarcerate teens for fifty years or more, which is what we are currently doing.

Stand with me. Together we can make a difference. Together we can get these kids help before they ruin their lives, the lives of their families, and the lives of their victims' families. We need to do our part to save innocent human beings and make our country and our world a better place. It's the least we can do.

I'd love to hear your thoughts, suggestions, questions, and comments. You can personally communicate with me by logging on to my Web site, www.PhilChalmers.com. There are also additional resources and more information for further study. I look forward to working with you to eliminate the problem of teen violence.

> TO FURTHER YOUR STUDY ON THE TOPIC OF TEEN MURDER, DON'T MISS PHIL'S BOOK, *THE ENCYCLOPEDIA OF TEEN KILLERS*, WHICH CAN BE PURCHASED AT PHILCHALMERS.COM.
> THIS BOOK CONTAINS FURTHER CASE DETAILS AND INFORMATION TOO GRAPHIC FOR MAINSTREAM PUBLICATION.

INDEX

INDEX

INDEX

NOTES

CHAPTER 1

1. Glenn Godfrey, "Woodham Apologizes," abcnews.com, November 12, 1997.
2. Howard N. Snyder and Melissa Sickmund, *Juvenile Offenders and Victims: 2006 National Report* (Washington, D.C.: U.S. Department of Justice, Office of Justice Programs, Office of Juvenile Justice and Delinquency Prevention, 2006).
3. Ibid.
4. *Indicators of School Crime and Safety: 2006*, U.S. Departments of Education and Justice, 2006.
5. *Indicators of School Violence and Safety report, 2007*, the National Center for Education Statistics (NCES), Institute of Education Sciences (IES) in the U.S. Department of Education, and the Bureau of Justice Statistics (BJS) in the U.S. Department of Justice.
6. See note 4 above.
7. Melissa Tyrrell, "Army Psychologist Fights for Peace," *York Daily Record*, November 6, 2000.
8. David Grossman, "Evolution of Weaponry," *Encyclopedia of Violence, Peace and Conflict* (New York: Academic Press, 2000).
9. *Wikipedia*, s.v. "Cody Posey" (article no longer available).
10. Ibid., s.v. "Brenda Ann Spencer," http://en.wikipedia.org/wiki/Brenda_Spencer.
11. Katherine Ramsland, with Trista Dashner, "The Allentown Massacres: The Third Statement," Tru TV Tru Crime Library, http://www.crimelibrary.com/notorious_murders/family/freeman_brothers/7.html.
12. Mark Arsenault, "Into another world," *Providence Journal* (projo.com), March 7, 2004, http://www.projo.com/extra/2004/craigprice/content/part1.htm.
13. "*Delaware v. Grossberg and Peterson*: Grossberg to Serve Two-and-Half Years; Peterson Receives Two-Year Sentence," Court TV Online, July 9 [1998], http://www.courttv.com/archive/trials/grossberg/070998.html.

CHAPTER 2

1. James Gabarino, in Sharon Begley, "The Anatomy of Violence," *Newsweek*, April 30, 2007, 1, http://www.newsweek.com/id/35257/page/1.
2. Ibid, 4.

3. William J. Bennett, *The Index of Leading Cultural Indicators* (n.p.: Touchstone, January 27, 1994).
4. Youth Suicide Prevention Program Web site, "Youth Suicide Frequently Asked Questions," http://www.yspp.org/aboutSuicide/suicideFAQ.htm. See answer to question 8.

CHAPTER 3

1. National Youth Violence Prevention Resource Center Web site, "Teen Substance Abuse and Violence Facts," under the heading "Substance Abuse and Violence" (esp. note 16), http://www.safeyouth.org/scripts/faq/substabuse.asp#16.
2. B. K. Eakman, *Cloning of the American Mind: Eradicating Morality Through Education* (n.p.: Hunting House Publishers, 1998).
3. W. E. Vine, *Vine's Expository Dictionary of New Testament Words*, s.v. "Sorcerer," provided on the Antioch Networks International Web site, http://www.antioch.com.sg/cgi-bin/bible/vines/get_defn.pl?num=2700.
4. Substance Abuse and Mental Health Services Administration, *Results from the 2005 National Survey on Drug Use and Health: National Findings* (Rockville, MD: Office of Applied Studies, 2006), NSDUH Series H-30, DHHS Publication No. SMA 06-4194), as cited in *2007 Florida Methamphetamine Control Strategy* (Office of Drug Control, Executive Office of the Governor: State of Florida), 11, http://www.flgov.com/pdfs/ODC-MethStrategy-Word.pdf.
5. Lloyd D. Johnston, Patrick M. O'Malley, and Jerald G. Bachman, *Monitoring the Future: National Results on Adolescent Drug Use* (The University of Michigan Institute for Social Research), December 2006.
6. Glenn Puitt, "Murder Trial: Detective Describes Stabbings," *Las Vegas Review-Journal,* June 3, 2005.
7. The Partnership for a Drug-Free America, The Partnership Attitude Tracking Study (PATS) Teens 2007 Report (2008), 16, chart 23, http://www.drugfree.org/Files/2007_Teen_Survey.
8. Peter Breggin, *Talking Back to Ritalin: What Doctors Aren't Telling You About Stimulants for Children* (Monroe, ME: Common Courage Press, 1998), 80–81.
9. Cooperative Institute for Medical Drug Dependence (Denmark, report), quoted on the Audiblox Web site article "Ritalin Side Effects," http://www.audiblox2000.com/learning_disabilities/ritalin.htm.
10. Dr. Fred Baughman, in "Death in the Woods," *Freedom Magazine,* http://www.freedommag.org/english/vol36i1/page04.htm.
11. National Institute on Drug Abuse, *Monitoring the Future Survey: National Results on Adolescent Drug Use: Overview of Key Findings 2005* (National Institutes of Health, U.S. Department of Health and Human Services), 44 (Table 1), http://www.monitoringthefuture.org/pubs/monographs/overview2005.pdf.
12. Taped interview between Kipland Philip Kinkel and Detective Al Warthen of the Springfield Police Department, May 21, 1998.

13. National Institute on Drug Abuse Web site, NIDA Drug Facts, "Treatment for Drug Abusers in the Criminal Justice System," http://www.drugabuse.gov/PDF/InfoFacts/CJTreatment06.pdf.

14. Debbie Kelley, "Cost of Drug Abuse: Drugtesting: Employers finding screenings ensure safer workplace," *Gazette* (Colorado Springs), April 17, 2006, Business, 37, http://daily.gazette.com/Repository/ml.asp?Ref=VGhlR2F6ZXR0ZS8yMDA2LzA0LzE3I0FyMDM7MDA=&Mode=HTML&Locale=english-skin-custom.

15. *Principles of Drug Abuse Treatment: A Research-Based Guide,* National Institutes of Health Publication No. 00-4180 (National Institute on Drug Abuse, U.S. Department of Health and Human Services, 1999), http://www.nida.nih.gov/PODAT/PODAT6.html#FAQ8.

CHAPTER 4

1. Mark Schone, "*The Matrix* Defense," *Boston Globe,* November 9, 2003.

2. Nancy Gibbs, "The Columbine Tape," *Time,* December 20, 1999.

3. "Journal: Columbine Attack Planned for a Year," *TheDenverChannel.com,* December 5, 2001, http://www.thedenverchannel.com/news/1103402/detail.html.

4. Johanna Schneller, "Hungry for Blood? Gore Porn's for You," *Globe and Mail,* October 31, 2003.

5. Gene Edward Veith, "Escalating Depravity," *World Magazine,* April 8, 2006.

6. Plugged In (a movie review Web site), "*Scream III*" Focus on the Family, http://www.pluggedinonline.com/movies/movies/a0000516.cfm.

7. Ibid.

8. "Girl Found Guilty of Hanging of Teen," *CJ Online National News,* January 29, 1999.

9. American Academy of Pediatrics, "Policy Statement," *Pediatrics* 108, no. 5 (November 2001):1222–26, http://aappolicy.aappublications.org/cgi/content/full/pediatrics;108/5/1222.

10. American Medical Association, "American Medical Association House of Delegates, Resolution: 424 (A-05)," http://www.ama-assn.org/meetings/public/annual05/424a05.doc.

11. *Kerrang Magazine,* July 26, 2003.

12. Geordie Greig, "Rat-a-tat of Gangsta Rap Is Sick, Say Blacks," *Sunday Times,* November 28, 1993.

13. Gil Kaufman, "Officials: Up to 20 Students May Have Ties to Red Lake Plot" (MTV News), April 4, 2005, on VH1 Web site, http://www.vh1.com/news/articles/1499494/04042005/id_0.jhtml.

14. Ibid.

15. Alison Motluck, "TV Viewing Linked to Adult Violence," *NewScientist.com,* March 28, 2002, http://www.newscientist.com/article/dn2109.

16. Ibid.

17. Christina Glaubke, Patti Miller, et al., "Fair Play? Violence, Gender and Race in Video Games," *Children Now,* December 2001.

18. Cathy Scott-Clark and Adrian Levy, "Fast Forward into Trouble," *Guardian*, June 14, 2003, http://www.guardian.co.uk/theguardian/2003/jun/14/weekend7. weekend2.

19. Ibid.

20. Brandon S. Centerwall, "Television and Violence: The Scale of the Problem and Where to Go from Here," *Journal of the American Medical Association*, June 10, 1992.

21. Fox Butterfield, "Seeds of Murder Epidemic: Teen-age Boys with Guns," *New York Times*, October 19, 1992, http://query.nytimes.com/gst/fullpage.html?res=9 E0CEEDC1339F93AA25753C1A964958260.

22. Mark Bonokowski, "The Warriors Re-Released Amid Violence," *Toronto Sun*, October 7, 2005.

23. Ken Kolker, "Police Curious About Similarities Between Deadly Beating and Video Game," *Grand Rapids Press*, December 8, 2002.

24. Ibid.

25. Douglass C. Perry, "Manhunt," http://ps2.ign.com/articles/440/440887p4.html.

26. "Media Violence May Affect Children's Minds," June 10, 2005, http://www.webmd. com/parenting/news/20050610/media-violence-may-affect-childrens-minds.

27. American Academy of Pediatrics, "Joint Statement on the Impact of Entertainment Violence on Children Congressional Public Health Summit July 26, 2000," http://www.aap.org/advocacy/releases/jstmtevc.htm.

28. Lawrie Mifflin, "Many Researchers Say Link Is Already Clear on Media and Youth Violence," May 9, 1999, *New York Times*, http://query.nytimes.com/gst/ fullpage.html?res=9E05E2DD173FF93AA35756C0A96F958260.

29. "Media Violence Does Affect Children, Medical Groups Say," July 26, 2000, http://www.webmd.com/news/20000726/media-violence-does-affect-children-medical-groups-say.

30. Radiological Society of North America, "Violent Video Games Leave Teenagers Emotionally Aroused," *ScienceDaily*, November 29, 2006, http://www. sciencedaily.com/releases/2006/11/061128140804.htm.

31. K. Browne and C. Hamilton-Giachritsis, "The Influence of Violent Media on Children and Adolescents: A Public-Health Approach," *Lancet*, 2005, 365:702–10.

32. Federal Trade Commission Web site, "Undercover Shop Finds Decrease in Sales of M-Rated Video Games to Children (Results from the 2005 Nationwide Undercover Shop Demonstrate Need for Continuing Improvement), March 30, 2006, http://www.ftc.gov/opa/2006/03/videogameshop.shtm.

33. Burt Helm and Carlos Bergfeld, "Congress, Stop Playing Games," *Business Week*, June 15, 2006, http://www.businessweek.com/technology/content/jun2006/ tc20060615_326390.htm.

34. Liza Mundy, "Do You Know Where Your Children Are?" *Washington Post*, November 16, 2003, W-12, http://www.washingtonpost.com/wp-dyn/content/ article/2003/11/16/AR2005032304861.html (online p. 1).

35. Ibid., online page 5.

CHAPTER 5

1. Mark Ames, "Virginia Tech: Is the Scene of the Crime the Cause of the Crime?," AlterNet, April 20, 2007, http://www.alternet.org/story/50758/?page=entire.
2. Dan Olweus, quoted on the Northeastern School District (Manchester, PA) Web site, *Spring Forge Intermediate Bullying Handbook*, http://www.nesd.k12. pa.us/Spring_Forge/Bullying%20Handbook.htm.
3. National Center for Education Statistics, *Indicators of School Crime and Safety: 2007, Executive Summary* (U.S. Department of Education, Institute of Education Sciences, http://nces.ed.gov/programs/crimeindicators/ crimeindicators2007.
4. Mental Health Association Web site, "Factsheet: Bullying: What to Do About It," http://www.nmha.org/index.cfm?objectid=CA866DBF-1372-4D20- C817AE97DDF77E4E.
5. Ibid.
6. Miya Omori, "Bullying: A New Sense of Need in the US Educational System," Child Research Net Web site, April 13, 2001, http://www.childresearch.net/ cgi-bin/topics/column.pl?no=00106&page=1.
7. Candy J. Cooper, "Cyberbullies Stalking Online Playground," *Record* (Bergen County, NJ), April 21, 2004, http://www.cyberbullying.org/Cyberbullies_ Stalking_Online_Playground_April_21_2004.html.
8. Amy Harmon, "Internet Gives Teenage Bullies Weapons to Wound from Afar," *New York Times*, August 26, 2004.
9. iSafe Web site, "Cyber Bullying: Statistics and Tips," http://www.isafe.org/ channels/sub.php?ch=op&sub_id=media_cyber_bullying.
10. Harmon, "Internet Gives Teenage Bullies Weapons to Wound from Afar."
11. David Cullen, "Goodbye, Cruel World," *Salon.com*, December 14, 1999, http:// www.salon.com/news/feature/1999/12/14/videos/.
12. Sue Ann Pressley, "A Bible Belt Town Searches for Answers," *Washington Post*, October 22, 1997, A03, http://www.washingtonpost.com/wp-srv/national/ longterm/juvmurders/stories/pearl.htm.
13. Tim Post, "Court Views McLaughlin Video Statement," *Minnesota Public Radio*, July 12, 2005.
14. Eve Kupersanim, "FBI Expert Says School Shooters Always Give Hints About Plan," *Psychiatric News*, June 21, 2002.

CHAPTER 6

1. John Lott, *More Guns, Less Crime*, 2nd ed. (Chicago: University Of Chicago Press, June 15, 2000).
2. James D. Wright and Peter H. Rossi, *Armed and Considered Dangerous: A Survey of Felons and Their Firearms* (New York: Aldine, 1986), 141, 145, 151.
3. Christopher Smart and Sheena McFarland, "Trolley Square: Gun-Rights Debate Gets Drawn into Aftermath," *Salt Lake Tribune*, February 14, 2007, http://www. sltrib.com/ci_5223644.

CHAPTER 7

1. "Teen Guilty in Mississippi School-Shooting Rampage," *CNN.com*, June 12, 1998, http://www.cnn.com/US/9806/12/school.shooting.verdict/.
2. Sue Lindsay, "Special Report: High-Risk Behavior," *Rocky Mountain News*, September 19, 2005.
3. Ibid.
4. Mike Ward, "U.S. Supreme Court Strikes Down Death Penalty for Juvenile Offenders," *American Statesman*, March 2, 2005, http://www.statesman.com/news/content/metro/yogurt/030205deathpenalty.html.
5. Death Penalty Information Center Web site, "Execution of Juveniles in the U.S. and Other Countries," http://www.deathpenaltyinfo.org/execution-juveniles-us-and-other-countries#execsworld.
6. Michael D. Kelleher, *When Good Kids Kill* (Westport, CT: Praeger, 1998).
7. Adam Liptak, "Jailed for Life After Crimes as Teenagers," *New York Times*, October 3, 2005, http://www.nytimes.com/2005/10/03/national/03lifers.html?pagewanted=2&ei=5088&en=7fbd46820fe91043&ex=1285992000&partner=rssnyt&emc=rss, page 2.
8. Robert Blecker, "A Poster Child for Us," *Judicature*, March/April 2006.
9. Liptak, "Jailed for Life."

CHAPTER 8

1. Brian McGrory, "Injustice for Almost All," *Boston Globe,* September 16, 2005, http://www.boston.com/news/local/massachusetts/articles/2005/09/16/injustice_for_almost_all/.

CHAPTER 9

1. Rich Hood, "Too Much Evil Breaking Out in Society," *Kansas City Star*, reprinted with permission on the Universal Light Institute Web site, http://www.universallight.org/too_much_evil.htm.
2. J. M. MacDonald, "The Threat to Kill," *American Journal of Psychiatry* 120 (1963):129–30.
3. John Douglas and Mark Olshaker, *The Anatomy of Motive: The FBI's Legendary Mindhunter Explores the Key to Understanding and Catching Violent Criminals* (New York: Pocket, 2000), 37.
4. Pat Brown, *Killing for Sport: Inside the Minds of Serial Killers* (n.p.: New Millennium Press, March 2003).
5. Harold Schechter, *The Serial Killer Files: The Who, What, Where, How, and Why of the World's Most Terrifying Murderers* ([New York?]: Ballantine Books, 2003), 162. Available online at http://www.scribd.com/doc/3258539/The-Serial-Killer-Files, 175.
6. Ibid., 26 (online p. 36).
7. Douglas and Olshaker, *The Anatomy of Motive*, 49.

8. See Morning Star Communications' *Son of Hope* (David Berkowitz) Web site, http://www.thesonofhope.com/.
9. Schechter, *Serial Killer Files* (online p. 36).
10. Harold Schechter, *The A to Z Encyclopedia of Serial Killers* (Pocket, 1997).
11. Elizabeth Hess, "Cruelty on the Couch," *New York* magazine, February 14, 2000, http://nymag.com/nymetro/news/crimelaw/features/2091/.
12. Schechter, *Serial Killer Files* (online p. 37).
13. Ibid.
14. "Around the Nation: Pennsylvania Teen-ager Is Given Death Sentence," *New York Times*, May 29, 1982, http://query.nytimes.com/gst/fullpage.html?res=9904 E7DD1138F93AA15756C0A964948260.

CHAPTER 10

1. Epigraph: Michael Newton, "Doing Doubles," TruTV Crime Library Web site, www.crimelibrary.com/serial_killers/predators/gerard_schaefer/6.html.
2. Albert M Drukteinis, "Contemporary Psychiatry: Serial Murder—The Heart of Darkness," *Psychiatric Annals,* 1992.

CHAPTER 11

1. *Seventh United Nations Survey of Crime Trends and Operations of Criminal Justice Systems* (Office on Drugs and Crime, Division for Policy Analysis and Public Affairs), http://www.unodc.org/pdf/crime/seventh_survey/7sc.pdf.
2. Matthias Armborst (Associated Press), "German Shoots 5 in His Former School," November 20, 2006, http://www.washingtonpost.com/wp-dyn/content/article/2006/11/20/AR2006112000175_pf.html.
3. Christopher Cobb and Bob Avery, *Rape of a Normal Mind* (Toronto: Paperjacks).
4. *Asiaweek.com* (CNN), http://www-cgi.cnn.com/ASIANOW/asiaweek/98/0320/feat8.html.
5. Reuters, "Boy Shoots Parents After Beating," October 19, 2004, http://www.cnn.com/2004/WORLD/europe/10/19/russia.shooting/index.html.
6. "Teen Killers Unable to Explain Savage Actions," *Namibian*, May 2000, www.namibian.com.na/Newstories/2000/May/News/0081D4F1C8.html.
7. "Sixteen-Year-Old Killers Sentenced to Life in Jail," *Daily Telegraph*, May 10, 2007, available on the *Australian* Web site, at http://www.theaustralian.news.com.au/story/0,25197,21704807-421,00.html.
8. Ibid.

CHAPTER 12

1. Jeffrey Ressner and Phil McGraw, "Ten Questions for Dr. Phil," *Time* magazine, September 13, 2004.

Phil Chalmers Recommends

Teen Crime Books

Babyface Killers, by Clifford Linedecker (St. Martin's Paperbacks, 1999). Includes a list of school shooters, as well as stories on several famous cases.

Child's Prey, by Jon Bellini (Pinnacle Books, 2001). In-depth story of Luke Woodham, the Pearl, Mississippi, school shooter.

Death of Innocence, by Peter Meyer (Berkeley, 1985). The story of the abduction and murder by teen killers Lois Hamlin and Jamie Savage in Vermont.

Die, Grandpa Die, by Dale Hudson (Pinnacle, 2006). The story of teen killer Christopher Pittman.

If You Really Loved Me, by Kevin McMurray (St. Martins, 2006). The story of teen killers Holly Harvey and Sandra Ketchum.

The Kids Next Door, by Gregory Morris (Morrow, 1985). An older book about teens killing their parents.

Kids Who Kill, by Charles Patrick Ewing (Avon Books, 1990). Numerous stories broken down into the different types of murder.

Killer Kids, by Don Lasseter (Pinnacle Books, 1998). Almost five hundred pages of stories of teen killers.

Killer Kids, by Clifford Linedecker (New York: New York, 1993). Good book discussing ten cases of teenagers who murdered their parents.

Murdered Innocents, by Corey Mitchell (Pinnacle, 2005). A book about the Yogurt Shop Murders in Austin, Texas.

Rattlesnake Romeo, by Joy Wellman (Pinnacle, 2005). The story of teen killers Adam Davis, Valessa Robinson, and Jon Whispel.

Savage Spawn, by Jonathan Kellerman (New York: Library of Contemporary Thought, Ballantine Publishing Group, 1999). This book explores the psychology behind kids who kill.

Sole Survivor: Children Who Murder Their Families, by Elliott Leyton (Seal Books, 1990). Covers only about five stories. Same author who wrote book *Hunting Humans.*

Someone Has to Die Tonight, by Jim Greenhill (Pinnacle, 2006). The story of the killing of a music teacher in Florida by four students.

Stop Teaching Our Kids to Kill, by Lt. Col. Dave Grossman and Gloria DeGaetano (Crown, 1999). Killing expert Dave Grossman talks about the connection between media violence and real-life violence.

Such Good Boys, by Tina Dirmann (St. Martins, 2005). The story of the Sopranos murder executed by Jason Bautista.

Teenage Rampage, by Antonio Mendoza (Virgin Books, 2002). Explores about sixteen cases of teen murder.

When Good Kids Kill, by Michael D. Kelleher (Praeger Publishers, 1998). Shocking, in-depth stories of "good kids" who kill.

SERIAL KILLER BOOKS

The Anatomy of Motive, by John Douglas (Pocket Books, 1999). Douglas explores the motive behind murder. Anything written by this guy is always fascinating.

I Have Lived in the Monster, by Robert Ressler (Thomas Dunne Books, 1997). My favorite book by a former-FBI criminal profiler.

Killing for Sport, by Pat Brown (New Millennium Press, 2003). The best book about serial killers I have ever read. Very informative and a must-have.

Mind Hunter, by John Douglas (Pocket Books, 1995). One of Douglas's first books and one of his best. Douglas is another former FBI criminal profiler.

The Serial Killer Files, by Harold Schechter (New York: Ballantine Books, 2003). Awesome history of serial killing, including information and details about the crimes and the motives and reasonings behind them. If you are trying to research serial killing, this one is for you.

The Unknown Darkness, by Gregg McCrary (William Morrow, 2003). Another former FBI criminal profiler delves into the world of serial killing.

Whoever Fights Monsters, by Robert Ressler (New York: St. Martins, 1992). Profiles of serial killers.

WEB SITES

BULLYING

www.bullyfree.com - Help with bullying in your school or community

www.nobully.org - A detailed examination of bullying

DRUG USE

www.FreeVibe.com - Facts on teen drug use

www.cadca.org - Community Anti-Drug Coalitions of America

www.Drugstrategies.org - Non-profit group fighting the drug problem in America

www.theantidrug.com - Great site for parents on talking to kids about drugs

www.ncadd.org - The National Council on Alcoholism and Drug Dependence

www.whitehousedrugpolicy.gov - Good facts and reports from the government

www.inhalants.org - Information and prevention of inhalants abuse

www.drugfree.org - Great information on drug use and effects

www.teeninstitute.org - Organization that teaches teens to resist drug use

www.kidshealth.org - Good health information for kids that is easy to understand

Media Discernment

www.PluggedInOnline.com - Music, movie, television, and video game reviews

www.ScreenIt.com - Movie review site

www.fradical.com - great Canadian Web site connecting media violence with murder

www.FamilyMediaGuide.com - Movie, television, and video game reviews

www.TheTVBoss.org - Ratings and the V-chip for television control

www.TVTurnoff.org - Information about dangers of mass consumption of television

www.Parentalguide.org - Parent media guide

www.MediaFamily.org - Video game reviews and more

Porn Addiction

www.xxxchurch.com - Porn filters and help for porn addiction

www.PureLifeMinistries.org - Outreach for those struggling with porn addition

Serial Killers

www.crimefan.com - Details on serial, spree, and teen killers

www.allserialkillers.com - Details and info on serial killers

Sexual Abuse

www.StopOffending.com - Assessment and treatment for sexual abuse and deviance

Suicide

www.jasonfoundation.com - Help and information on suicide

Teen Crime

www.PhilChalmers.com - My Web site

www.CrimeLibrary.com - The most comprehensive Web site on murder and crime www.crimenews2000.com - Crime news ticker with headlines across the world

www.LeopoldandLoeb.com - Interesting site about the first teen thrill killers

www.KariSable.com - Great crime site that details hundreds of stories and crimes

www.ncjrs.org - National Criminal Justice Reference Service

www.crime-free.org - Crime Free America

www.senate.gov - United States Senate

www.aclu.org - American Civil Liberties Union

www.ojp.usdoj.gov - United States Department of Justice

www.apa.org - American Psychological Association

www.ncpa.org - National Center for Policy Analysis

www.pbs.org - PBS Online

www.kanzafoundation.org - Juvenile Crime and Justice Research in Kansas

www.broadway.vera.org -Vera Institute of Justice

www.iir.com - The Institute for Inter-Government Research

www.rand.org - The RAND Corporation

www.ViolentKids.com - Forensic psychologist Dr. Helen Smith

www.SafeYouth.org - Working to help keep our kids safe

www.CrimeNews.info - Information and updates on crime stories

For additional resources and information, visit www.PhilChalmers.com.

THE LONGEST LIST
OF TEEN KILLERS EVER PRINTED

Here is what might possibly be the longest list ever published of teen killers. It is organized by the year of the killer's crime. I have personally interviewed and corresponded with many of the men and women featured in this section. To get the full details of the crimes listed below, and much more, see Phil's book, *The Encyclopedia of Teen Killers*, available at PhilChalmers.com.

1786—Hannah Ocuish

1872—Jesse Harding Pomeroy

May 24, 1924—Nathan Leopold and Richard Loeb

March 24, 1944—George Stinney

March 1951—Henry Lucas

January 21, 1958—Charles Starkweather

October 1960—Raymond Eugene Brown

August 1963—Edmund Kemper III

December 1968—Mary Bell and Norma Bell

1968—Jerry Lee Bellamy

December 30, 1974—Anthony Barbaro

May 4, 1976—Patricia Ann Columbo

October 1977—Terry Roach and Ronnie Mahaffey

February 22, 1978—Roger Needham

March 19, 1978—Willie Bosket

June 1978—Jeffrey Dahmer

January 29, 1979—Brenda Spencer

March 1, 1979—Kevin Hughes

October 26, 1979—Jay Kelly Pinkerton

March 20, 1980—Doil Edward Lane

August 28, 1980—Teresa Bickerstaff

September 3, 1980—Janice Buttrum

January 7, 1981—Kevin Stanford

February 5, 1981—Frederick Lynn and Garret Strong

May 1981—Jamie Savage and Louis Hamlin

July 26, 1981—Joseph Aulisio

October 31, 1981—Johnny Frank Garrett

November 3, 1981—Anthony Jacques Broussard

March 19, 1982—Patrick Lizotte

September 5, 1982—Gary Brown, Paul Everson, and Shane Kennedy

November 16, 1982—Richard Jahnke Jr.

January 23, 1983—William Wayne Thompson

January 28, 1983—James Earl Slaughter

January 1983—Jerry Ball

April 2, 1983—Marko Bey

June 14, 1983—Cindy Collier and Shirley Wolf

August 18, 1983—Ross Michael Carlson

August 27, 1983—Jory Kidwell

October 1983—Matthew Rosenberg

1983—Ronald Lampasi

January 17, 1984—Larry Swartz

March, 1984—Robert Lee Moody

April 2, 1984—Michael Smalley

June 15, 1984—Richard Kasso

September 8, 1984—Patrick DeGelleke

October 13, 1984—Torran Lee Meier

1984—Pamela Knuckles

1984—Stephen Hugueley

1984—Dale Whipple

January 4, 1985—Joseph Willey

January 15, 1985—John Morris, Alton Smith, Christopher Caldwell, and Eric Anderson

January 21, 1985—James Alan Kearbey

April 12, 1985—Ronald Ward

April 30, 1985—Dennis Ryan

April 1985—Britt Kellum

May 7, 1985—James McClure

May 26, 1985—Cayce Moore, Scott Davis, and Chris White

June 28, 1985—Robert Rosenkrantz

September 8, 1985—Sean Sellers

September 16, 1985—John Justice

October 1, 1985—Karen Severson and Laura Doyle

November 12, 1985—Shawn Milne

November 1985—David Ventiquattro

1985—Charles Rumbaugh

January 17, 1986—Louis Conner

January 21, 1986—James Alan Kearbey

February 2, 1986—Lloyd Gamble

February 5, 1986—Sean Pica and Cheryl Pierson

February 14, 1986—Robert Ward

February 17, 1986—Heidi Gasparovich and Matthew Gasparovich Jr.

February 27, 1986—Percy Lee

April 26, 1986—Ginger Turnmire

May 6, 1986—Charles Lorraine

August 31, 1986—Richard Cooey, Kenneth Horonetz, and Clint Dickens

September 20, 1986—William Owens

September 29, 1986—Sandy Shaw and Troy Kell

November 20, 1986—Rod Matthews

November 21, 1986—Austin Addison

December 4, 1986—Kristofer Hans

December 13, 1986—Wyley Gates

December 19, 1986—John Lester, Scott Kern, and Jason Ladone

January 1, 1987—Sean Stevenson

January 1987—Kristin Rice, Tamara Liggins, and Wayne Mialki

February 11, 1987—Tim Masters

February 24, 1987—Milton Jones and Theodore Simmons

March 2, 1987—Nathan Faris

March 22, 1987—Tim Erickson

May 25, 1987—Andrea "Cookie" Williams and Mario Garcia

April 25, 1987–August 15, 1987—Clinton Bankston Jr.

May 1987—Paula Cooper

June 1987—Craig Price

July 1987—Michael Boettlin Jr.

July 14, 1987—Timothy Cargle

August 5, 1987—Dennis Coleman

September 20, 1987—Michael Smalley

October 6, 1987—Alonzo Williams

October 12, 1987—Timothy Scott Sherman

November 5, 1987—Jimmy Iriel and Robert Mcilvain

December 1, 1987—Daniel LaPlante

December 6, 1987—Jim Hardy, Pete Roland, and Ron Clements

December 1987—Scott McKee and Dean McKee

January 15, 1988—Matthew Schrom and Anthony Holtorff

January 1988—Leslie Torres

February 8, 1988—Robert Demeritt and Jayson Moore

February 11, 1988—Jason Hartess

February 18, 1988—David Brom

April 19, 1988—Kenny Houseknecht

March 27, 1988—Derek Christopher Lincoln and Richard Greenway

June 25, 1988—William Shrubsall

September 26, 1988—James Wilson

October 12, 1988—Jon Cantero

October 18, 1988—Brian Houchin, Joseph Hallock, and Larry Allen

October 24, 1988—Mark Branch

November 8, 1988—Kenneth Kovzelove and Dennis Bencivenga

November 8, 1988—Marsha Urevich and Nicole Eisel

November 28, 1988—Daniel Yarbrough

December 6, 1988—Eugene Turley

December 16, 1988—Nicholas Elliott

1988—Timothy Scott Sherman

January 31, 1989—Anthony Pilato and Isaac Hill

March 13, 1989—Arva Betts

March 21, 1989—Brian Britton

March 23, 1989—Curtis Cooper

June 16, 1989—Steven Porell

July 12, 1989—Mark Grimm

September 29, 1989—Shawn David Jackson

February 28, 1990—David Leon Wilson

March 17, 1990—Billy Shane Willingham

March 24, 1990—Phillip Negrete, Jammi Reimier, and Sam Archer

July 21, 1990—Katherine Maria Telemachos

July 27, 1990—Adriel Simpson

August 27, 1990—Curtis Collins

September 27, 1990—Christopher Carrion and Leigh Ann Zaepfel

October 28, 1990—Steven Pigg, Curtis Burke, and Carl Purvis

January 16, 1991—Jose Loza

March 4, 1991—Shawn Novak

May 28, 1991—Guillermo Bustos and Michael Loretto

June 27, 1991—Roderick Davie

August 6, 1991—Gavin Mandin

August 31, 1991—Todd Davilla

September 4, 1991—April Leigh Barber

November 16, 1991—Johnnie "Ken" Register

November 23, 1991—Taryn Lagrome

November 1991—Jason Kennedy

December 6, 1991—Robert Springsteen IV

1991—Amy Ellwood

January 11, 1992—Toni Lawrence, Hope Rippey, Lauri Tackett, and Melinda Loveless

January 23, 1992—Jermarco Hicks

January 26, 1992—Timothy Kane, Alvin Morton, and Bobby Garner

February 24, 1992—Brian Tate

March 12, 1992—Kristi Anne Koslow

April 10, 1992—Brian Arthur Tate

April 11, 1992—Ronald Ray Howard

June 10, 1992—Gregory Devon Gibson

September 2, 1992—Kenneth Laird

December 14, 1992—Wayne Lo

1992—Shannon Garrison, Melissa Garrison, and Allen Robert Goul

1992—Stephanie Wernick

January 18, 1993—Gary "Scott" Pennington

January 30, 1993—Richard Henyard and Alfonza Smalls

February 2, 1993—Shem S. McCoy

February 12, 1993—Robert Thompson and Jon Venables

February 22, 1993—Robert Heard

May 5, 1993—Damien Wayne Echols, Jason Baldwin, and Jesse Lloyd Misskelley

May 6, 1993—James Phillip Bridson

May 24, 1993—Jason Michael Smith

May 1993—Andy Merritt

May 1993—Mighty T. Howell and Danyelle T. Wiley

June 14, 1993—Andrew DeYoung and David Haggerty

June 24, 1993—Sean Derrick O'Brien, Efrain Perez, Raul Villarreal, Peter Cantu, and Jose Medellin

June 1993—Victor Brancaccio

August 2, 1993—Eric Smith

August 1993—Shannon Musgraves

September 5, 1993—Jose Ignacio Monterrubio

September 9, 1993—Christopher Simmons and Charlie Benjamin

October 1993—Gerard McCra

December 27, 1993—Raymond Levi Cobb

January 23, 1994—Caryon Johnson, Kunta Sims, Steven Johnson, Sylvester Berry, and Calvin Smith

February 4, 1994—Michael Brown, Bernadette Setser, and Jeremy Rose

February 4, 1994—Ricardo Punsalan

February 22, 1994—Trace Duncan and Kenneth Loggins

February 23, 1994—Christopher Golly

March 16, 1994—Sean Sword, Patrick Weatherwax, Gregorio Riojas, and Eugene Pickard Jr.

April 10, 1994—Michael Haywood, Daniel Robago, Jason Brumwell, and Johl Brock

April 12, 1994—James Osmanson

May 26, 1994—Clay Shrout

August 19, 1994—Bobby Terrell Sheppard

September 21, 1994—Robert Alan Shields Jr.

October 23, 1994—Stephen Virgil McGilberry

October 30, 1994—Nathan Martinez

December 29, 1994—Gueneviere "Wendy" Gardner and James Evans

January 23, 1995—John Sirola

February 19, 1995—Jose Noey Martinez

February 27, 1995—Bryan Freeman, David Freeman, and Nelson "Ben" Birdwell

March 2, 1995—Jeffrey Howorth

March 5, 1995—Jason Lewis

March 7–8, 1995—Ben Darras and Sarah Edmondson

March 10, 1995—Nathan Joe Ramirez and Johnathan Grimshaw

April 17, 1995—Jasen Shane Busby

July 22, 1995—Joseph Fiorella, Jacob Delashmutt, and Royce Casey

July 23, 1995—Edward O'Brien Jr.

August 29, 1995—Keith Johnson

August 1995—Nicholaus McDonald and Brian Bassett

September 30, 1995—Nathan Brooks

October 7, 1995—Raymond Aiolentuna

October 12, 1995—Toby Sincino

October 17, 1995—Brian Pruitt

November 10, 1995—Jeremy Bach

November 15, 1995—Jamie Rouse

December 4, 1995—David Graham and Diane Zamora

February 2, 1996—Joshua Jenkins

February 2, 1996—Barry Loukaitis

February 22, 1996—Danny Connolly

March 25, 1996—Joseph Stanley Burris, Jonathan Dean Moore, and Anthony Gene Rutherford

April 30, 1996—Kevin Foster, Derek Shields, Christopher Black, and Peter Magnotti

May 16, 1996—Jeremy Hernandez

May 24, 1996—Lecresha Murray

September 1996—Jennifer Lee Tombs

October 16, 1996—Gena Lawson

November 12, 1996—Amy Grossberg and Brian Perterson Jr.

November 25, 1996—Rod Ferrell

December 2, 1996—David Dubose Jr.

January 3, 1997—Alex Baranyi and David Anderson

January 21, 1997—Michael Lewis

January 27, 1997—Tronneal Mangum

February 6, 1997—Robert Dingman and Jeffrey Dingman

February 19, 1997—Evan Ramsey

March 22, 1997—Mark Antony Duke and Brandon Samra

April 19, 1997—Thomas Koskovich and Jason Vreeland

April 21, 1997—Justin Fuller

May 22, 1997—Daphne Abdela and Christopher Vasquez

May 25, 1997—Jeremy Strohmeyer

June 6, 1997—Melissa Drexler

July 3, 1997—Jimmy Hernandez

September 23, 1997—Kevin Salvador Golphin and Tilmon Golphin

September 27, 1997—Sam Manzie

September 29, 1997—Todd Rizzo

October 1, 1997—Luke Woodham

October 19, 1997—Alan Walter, Dorothy Hallas, Jeff Boyette, June Seger, and Maggie Bennett

October 25, 1997—Son Vu Khai Tran

October 29, 1997—Nathaniel Abraham

December 1, 1997—Michael Carneal.

January 14, 1998—Mario Padilla and Samuel Ramirez

January 21, 1998—Kenneth Parr

January 29, 1998—Henry Lee Dreyer and Daniel Whitlow

February 9, 1998—Christopher Churchill

February 15, 1998—Michael Wayne Hall

March 10, 1998—Jeffrey Franklin

March 24, 1998—Andrew Golden and Mitchell Johnson

April 24, 1998—Andrew Wurst

April 28, 1998—Joseph Martinez

May 10, 1998—Jessica Holtmeyer and Aaron James Straw

May 19, 1998—Jacob Lee Davis

May 21, 1998—Kipland "Kip" Kinkel

May 30, 1998—Kyle Ray and Colby Becker

June 27, 1998—Valessa Robinson, Adam Davis, and Jon Whispel

July 26, 1998—Josh Cain and Trevor Walraven

August 8, 1998—Carlton Aker Turner

September 28, 1998—Raymond Gomez

August 19, 1998—Terrance Hunt

October 11, 1998—Zachary Witman

November 3, 1998—Joshua Phillips

November 29, 1998—Ray Jasper

December 15, 1998—Milton Wuzael Mathis

January 6, 1999—Catherine Jones

January 17, 1999—Christipher Huerstel and Kajornsak Prasertphong

January 1999—Patrick Boykin

February 3, 1999—Bruce Williams

April 20, 1999—Dylan Klebold and Eric Harris

May 27, 1999—Clayton Gordon

May 31, 1999—Terrell Yarbrough and Nathan Herring

July 28, 1999—Lionel Tate

July 1999—Mario Padilla and Samuel Ramirez

August 20, 1999—Whitney Lee Reeves

December 1999—Laird Stanard

February 29, 2000—Dedrick Owens

March 10, 2000—Darrell Ingram

July 22, 2000—Christy Phillips

August 26, 2000—Jonathan Mcneill, Dale Stewart, and Dan Angus

January 27, 2001—Robert Tulloch and James Parker

February 23, 2001—David Attias

March 5, 2001—Charles Andrew Williams

March 21, 2001—Matthew Rooy

May 22, 2001—Scott Lang

May 26, 2000—Nathaniel Brazill

June 4, 2001—Irving Alvin Davis

July 28, 2001—Jorge Alfredo Salinas

November 26, 2001—Derek King and Alex King

November 28, 2001—Christopher Pittman

December 31, 2001—David Pallister

February 4, 2002—Llewelyn James

February 10, 2002—Gorman Roberts

July 2, 2002—Derrick Dewayne Charles

September 2, 2002—Richard Aaron Cobb

October 2002—Lee Boyd Malvo

November 2, 2002—Dustin Lynch

December 8, 2002—Blake Walker

January 2, 2003—Keith Munden

January 4, 2003—Wade Logan

January 14, 2003—Jason Bautista and Matthew Montejo

January 22, 2003—Beau Maestas and Monique Maestas

February 17, 2003—Josh Cooke

February 26, 2003—David Hightower

March 8, 2003—Marcus Sellers and Andre Conley

April 24, 2003—Amber Rose Riley and Jason Lamar Harris

May 30, 2003—Justina Morley, Edward Batzig, Domenic Coia, and Nicolas Coia

June 7, 2003—Devin Darnell Thompson

June 25, 2003—William Buckner and Joshua Buckner

June 27, 2003—Ryan McCrickard

July 31, 2003—Gary Hirte

August 21, 2003—Joshua Goldman and Jenson Hankins

September 2, 2003—Sarah Johnson

September 17, 2003—Larketa Collier and Sharon Patterson

September 24, 2003—Jason John McLaughlin.

September 24, 2003—Gary Wayne Laquier and Margaret Fleissner

November 26, 2003—Jonathan Williams and Nicole Governale

December 8, 2003—Zachary Eggers

January 29, 2004—Lonnie Hall

February 3, 2004—Michael Hernandez

February 13, 2004—Charles Bryant and Nayquan Miller

February 16, 2004—Steven Tomporowski

April 21, 2004—Valentino Mitchell Arenas

April 22, 2004—Bryan Christopher Sturm

May 13, 2004—David Harris

May 21, 2004—Tristan Williams

May 28, 2004—Nakisha Waddell and Anastasia Belcher

June 16, 2004—Lonnie Bassett

June 17, 2004—Nathaniel Geebro

June 29, 2004—Kenneth Meeks and James Arthur Johnson

July 5, 2004—Cody Posey

August 2, 2004—Holly Harvey and Sandy Ketchum

October 10, 2004—Aaron Clark

November 13, 2004—Anthony Romanelli and Joseph Mumma

November 14, 2004—Rachelle Waterman

November 22, 2004—Desmond Keels

December 27, 2004—Christopher Alexander

January 5, 2005—Kurtis Graves

January 21, 2005—Sarah Kolb and Cory Gregory

February 27, 2005—Zachary Gibian

March 2, 2005—Jason Clinard

March 21, 2005—Jeff Weise

March 31, 2005—Tracey Dyess

April 24, 2005—Christopher James Dankovich

April 29, 2005—Adam Sapikowski

May 29, 2005—Scott Moody

July 2, 2005—Darran Samuel

July 30, 2005—Jonathan Zarate

October 15, 2005—Scott Dyleski

October 19, 2005—Andrew Tanner

November 8, 2005—Kenny Bartley

November 13, 2005—David Ludwig

January 19, 2006—John Odgren

February 2, 2006—Jacob Robida

July 8, 2006—Matthew McCombs and Sean Brown

July 23, 2006—Zachariah Blanton

August 4, 2006—Jeremy Hauck

August 30, 2006—Alvaro Rafael Castillo

September 2, 2006—John Messiha, Daniel Betancourt, and Travis King

November 23, 2006—Kendra Jones

November 29, 2006—Eric Hainstock

February 4, 2007—Bryan Grove, Tess Damm, Jared Sajal Guy, and Jared Smith

February 11, 2007—Caleb Sosa

February 12, 2007—Sulejmen Talovic

March 14, 2007—Connor Wood

May 6, 2007—Patrick Williams

June 22, 2007—Nicolas Castillo and Todd Hoke

July 29, 2007—Tabitha Messina and Carlos Christopher

July 30, 2007—Rachel Booth

ABOUT THE AUTHOR

Phil as Police Chaplain of the New Philadelphia Police Department.

Phil Chalmers has been researching, writing, and speaking all across America and abroad about youth culture, trends, and teen murder for more than twenty years. He has spoken to more than one million students on topics such as teen sex and abstinence, drug and alcohol abuse, teen violence, suicide, and media discernment. Phil's life purpose is to help teens make wise choices by teaching them about truth and consequences. For the last ten years, he has devoted his time to an in-depth study of teen crime and has established communication with more than two hundred adult and teen killers for their stories and "expert" advice.

Phil has authored two books, including *Can You Handle the Truth?* He has produced videos including the popular series *True Lies,* which has been viewed by more than one million people. He is invited to speak at about one hundred events per year and has made many media appearances, including *The Montel Williams Show* and *The Howard Stern Show.* Phil has presented live seminars in every state in America and has appeared on radio and television stations abroad. He has been featured in hundreds of newspapers and magazines including *People.* Phil resides in Ohio.

Consistently rated highly as a speaker, Phil Chalmers is available to educate and inform both small and large groups on all aspects of teen murder and school violence. He is available to speak at such venues as high schools, middle schools, college campuses, law enforcement conferences, local police and sheriff agencies, law enforcement academies, church groups, youth conferences, or wherever an energetic and life-changing speaker is welcome. Phil offers two separate seminars: "20/20 Blind," a live presentation about destructive decisions made by teens, is geared more toward teens and youth workers. The other seminar, "Inside the Mind of a Teen Killer," is geared toward law enforcement, teachers, and college campuses. It takes readers of this book to the next level, allowing them to see crime scene photos, watch interrogation videos, and find out how these crimes were stopped, solved, and what investigators would have done differently.

For more information about Phil Chalmers, to purchase his products, to join his street team, to check out his videos and photos, or to contact him, log on to his Web site at PhilChalmers.com or TeenKillers.com. You can also catch him on MySpace at MySpace.com/PhilChalmers.

CPSIA information can be obtained at www.ICGtesting.com
Printed in the USA
LVOW111120220412

278601LV00002B/4/P